TRUMPSPEAK

Bérengère Viennot

TRUMPSPEAK

Bérengère Viennot

Translated by

Susan Pickford

Contra Mundum Press   New York · London · Melbourne

Translation © 2020
Susan Pickford; *La langue
de Trump* © Editions Les
Arènes, Paris, 2019

First Contra Mundum
Press edition 2020.

Library of Congress
Cataloguing-in-Publication
Data

Viennot, Bérengère, 1973–
[La langue de Trump.
English.]
Trumpspeak / Bérengère
Viennot;
Translated from the French
by Susan Pickford

— 1ˢᵗ Contra Mundum Press
Edition

118 pp., 4.37×7 in.

ISBN 9781940625430

I. Viennot, Bérengère.
II. Title.
III. Pickford, Susan.
IV. Title.

2020946369

For Bonnie & Joshua

It is a sad thing when men have neither enough intelligence to speak well nor enough sense to hold their tongues.
 —Jean de La Bruyère

I know the best words.
 —Donald J. Trump

Table of Contents

Preface

When I wrote this book, Donald Trump was eighteen months into his presidency, and the whole world seemed to be struggling to find the words to describe the Trump phenomenon. Every time he opened his mouth, politicians, journalists, and amateur Trump-watchers gawped — or shook with outrage — at the apparently thoughtless language of the oddity in the Oval Office, an aberration among presidents who cared little for grand speeches and politically expedient prevarication and whose interviews and speeches seemed curiously underprepared.

The forty-fifth president of the United States has been the cause of much ink spillage, virtual or otherwise, on social media, in the press, and in print. Over the past four years, over 1,200 books have been written on him and his administration, some by well-known figures such as Michael Wolff, Bob Woodward, and James Comey, others by less familiar names — ex-Trumpites disappointed in, and often fired by, the man himself.[1] Then there are books by his admirers in praise of his leadership, and most recently, the tell-all, tear-him-down exposé by his niece Mary.

A few weeks out from the election that will either see Trump keep the reins for another four years or leave office, the broad lines of the argument I made back in the summer of 2018 have grown even clearer. While most analysts focused, logically enough, on his politics, I drew on my experience in journalism and my work as a translator to explore Trump's use of language. It quickly became clear to me that beneath the public persona of the straight-talking, straight-shooting big guy, Donald Trump, shored up by his

1. See Elizabeth A. Harris and Alexandra Alter, "Trump Books Keep Coming, and Readers Can't Stop Buying," *The New York Times* (Aug. 31, 2020).

close associates and family, was beginning to build a fortress for the faithful, its foundations underpinned by a vision of America built on violence and hatred.

Trumpspeak, his most effective weapon, also turned out to be one of the most under-analyzed from the outset. Analysts and opponents had so much fun pointing and laughing at his clumsy use of language that they were too quick to conclude that he was just an amateur, a chaotic reality TV huckster with no vision or plan for the future of his country. He didn't seem credible, so they gave him little credence.

But words bear witness to the realities we all bear deep within us, and the reality Trump's words have long pointed to is horrifying. It is a profoundly painful experience to take our fingers out of our ears and listen to words that claim there are "very fine people" on both sides (neo-Nazis and anti-racism protesters); words that demand the death penalty and walls to divide people; words that brutally crush social conflicts stirred by racism; words that refuse to condemn killers and seek to shift the responsibility for a global pandemic onto a country and its people rather than face up to the truth of a public health *&* social catastrophe on American soil.

Because Trump never bothered to wrap his speeches up in pretty words and pat political catch-phrases, we never took him seriously. And while half the world mocked his ignorance and his constant digressions and took amused, superior offense at his ostentatious displays of admiration for the worst tyrants of the age, he was busy applying the old adage "divide and rule" and digging an ever deeper chasm between two Americas, without the slightest suggestion of how it might be filled in again. His vulgar, aggressive outbursts, which early in his presidency brought out in us incredulous laughter, have since revealed the sheer force of personality of a man who has truly grasped that if the country were to come together again, it would be in opposition to him.

Trumpspeak is the language that began building an alt-reality straight after the inauguration and that, right down to the wire on his re-election campaign, is working to foster denial in an entire segment of the population, desperate to believe in his version of the American Dream. Trumpspeak is the language that lets his supporters at the Republican convention string together lie after lie to feed to those ready to settle for a black-and-white world where Trump stakes his claim to be the ultimate righter of wrongs, the fireman on call to put out a blaze he set alight himself. It is the language used in self-justification by all the Americans at the end of their tether who resort to violence, their consciences stilled by the moral inertia of the man who supposedly embodies the unity of their great nation.

Four years into his time in office, we can now see that Trumpspeak was the window dressing that let Trump and his clique nudge the entire apparatus of state ever further right; a smokescreen to confuse those who refused to see him as in any way credible. Deliberately or otherwise, it placed a grotesque facade at the forefront of American political life, with the up-shot that Americans as a whole, and Democrats in particular, refused to take him seriously. In fact, so busy were we all ridiculing a man who can barely read, who is staggeringly ignorant, and seems not to know how to behave in public that we all dropped our guard. We should have mistrusted a language that has proved to be a grave threat for American democracy and for the wider Western world that has always looked to the United States for inspiration. We should have mistrusted Trumpspeak.

Hangover

For the millions of Americans who, prior to November 2016, never believed for a second that a narcissistic, sexist, racist, ignorant billionaire could reach the highest office in the land after George Washington, Abraham Lincoln, and Theodore Roosevelt, it's been the longest hangover in history.

It was a violently unexpected blow for many people across the United States and round the world. I'm a press translator, and on November 8, 2016, I was ready to stay up late in case any last-minute pre-election translations landed in my inbox before the results were expected early the next morning. Though some misgivings did sneak in during the weeks leading up to D-Day, I was quietly confident: a Trump victory was unthinkable. Not just because he wasn't up to the job or because personally I didn't want him, not just because I really, really liked the idea of the first female POTUS straight after a Black president, but simply because the concept was totally, absolutely, unarguably ridiculous.

By the time I went to bed at two that morning, two states had posted their initial results: Kentucky had voted for Donald Trump by 72.7 %, Indiana by 69.3%. OK, I thought to myself, Indiana has long been staunchly Republican and Kentucky has been leaning to the right since the early 2000s. It'll be a close-run thing, but Hillary will pull it out of the bag. There can only be one winner in this fight. Night, all.

I woke up to the bitter taste of defeat.

For me as a translator, Trump's election was a seismic shift. On a personal level, because I'm no fan of the man himself (and I find it even harder to hide my dislike, as you will see), and because I'm interested enough in international politics to have some inkling of what a potential disaster his rise to power was. And on a professional level, too, because the election forced a sudden, violent change in my working practices, pushing me out of the comfort zone I'd been cozily ensconced in since Barack Obama came to power in November 2008, with no sweeteners to make up for it. For, like this strange presidency from the world of reality TV, utter ostentation, and overblown ego, Trump-speak — the raw material I work with — turned out to belong to a whole new realm that was both the cause and effect of the advent of a new America.

Daring to Translate Trump

My translation career brings me into contact with the entire spectrum of international current affairs, and depending on the commissions my clients give me, I have translated all sorts of texts about the various political upheavals that have shaken the planet since the turn of the millennium. The work is as fascinating as it is poorly paid, putting me in the category of people whose career is their calling in life. Practically an artist. The people who love what they do so much that they put up with the invisibility and social and financial disregard that comes with the territory.

The translator (usually a woman — there *are* some male translators out there, I know, but hey, they can write their own books) is invisible by nature. Her task is to transpose a message from language (say, English) into another (say, French). And let me stop a moment and offer up a silent word of thanks for all the translators who will have to translate this book into Uzbek, Serbo-Croat, and Nahuatl. I know you're out there, even if no one else does.

Contrary to the received opinions that all my colleagues run up against throughout their careers, translation isn't just a matter of translating words, and it's not something that just anyone can do. It takes more than speaking two languages, or having a good dictionary, or being on first-name terms with the son of the British Council cleaning lady.

Translation is about transmitting a *message* from one language to another. That takes several steps, none of which can be skipped. First of all, you have to understand the source text. Seems obvious? Well, there's more to it than meets the eye. Understanding a text or a speech means more than just knowing each of the individual words. A text is far more than the sum of its semantic parts. (Actually, the toaster that hammers on the alluring clam will not diminish the bones of my aunt's bicycle. You know all the words in this sentence, yet its meaning escapes you. Don't worry, me too. Words, words, words....)

For a text to exist, it must above all have a meaning, a referent, a message to transmit. Otherwise it's just a list of words — which can perfectly well be translated, of course, but whose semantic interest is open to question (with a special dispensation for the poems of Jacques Prévert). Translating lists might be useful in the field of technology, to describe the parts of a machine or draw up an inventory. In political translation, which is what we're talking about here, the aim is to recreate a coherent human discourse bearing a message destined for transmission.

Another prerequisite for translating a text or speech is being thoroughly familiar with the author's language, culture, and past experience — in short, knowing who the speaker is and having as much background on him as you can. Why? Because of a concept that has taken on a mystical dimension in the translation community, without which we are nothing: *context*. Just as an individual is influenced and shaped by their surroundings, words, sentences, entire speeches are meaningful only in context. Because the same sentence will mean something quite different when spoken by an American billionaire having achieved the highest office or, say, a gym coach or a physiotherapist.

Translation is the art of recreating the intellectual and affective sensations felt by readers of the source text in your own language (good translators always work into their mother tongue). The same word doesn't always reflect the same realities in different languages, even when it seems wholly basic and unambiguous. For instance, say "fromage" (cheese) to a Frenchman and he'll conjure up the image of a camembert (or maybe a comté, OK). The concept will take on an everyday familiarity, deeply anchored in French history. Now say "cheese" to an American, and he'll picture an industrial, cellophane-wrapped foodstuff that triggers a whole new range of sensations and images (and as for the smell, well, let's not even go there). The same goes for pomodoro / tomato, Italy vs. England, say, or for things that aren't food. "Université," a word that is easy to translate, would be "university" in Britain or "college" in the States, covering very different realities on the ground. In most cases, there is a way to come up with an equivalent meaning that reaches beyond the form and appearance of words. This work, reformulating words, aims to recreate the message as faithfully as possible, taking into account all of the aspects I've just been talking about. *That's* what a translator does.

Let's look at an example. July 14, 2017. Trump is on a brief visit to Paris for Bastille Day, the French national holiday, and is introduced to the French First Lady, Brigitte Macron. He exclaims, "You're in such good shape!" Then he turns to the French president and repeats, "She's in such good physical shape!" Then he turns back to Mme Macron once more and concludes with a triumphant "Beautiful!"

Many French media outlets translated "You're in such good shape" as "Vous êtes en super forme!" (You're in great condition!). And, word for word, that is more or less right. And that might be the proper translation if the individual saying those words was another person in another context: a physiotherapist to his patient, a gym coach admiring his new client, a man to his wife's mother — there's no shortage of possibilities.

In this precise instance, however, "You're in such good shape" cannot be translated as "Vous êtes en super forme." Because if you take into consideration the context, the moment, and the speaker's personality, i.e. the fact that this is an openly sexist man who boasts of grabbing women by the pussy and despises them to the point of hinting that a hostile journalist is on her period, a man capable of denigrating a rival candidate for the Republican nomination because he finds her unattractive,[1] and who refused to get his wife pregnant unless she promised to get her body back afterwards — in short, when you are familiar with the man himself, macho to the core, you have to take it into account and a literal translation becomes impossible.

Another key parameter: who is the POTUS talking to? He makes no bones about his preference for beautiful young women, to the point that he has even said that if Ivanka Trump weren't his daughter he'd date her himself. He's one of those men who think only young women can be beautiful. Past a certain age, she goes beyond her sell-by date, becomes invisible, and is no longer labeled "desirable."

Mme Macron was well into her sixties when she drew such fulsome praise from Trump. An old lady who still looks like a woman, wow, did you ever! That must have rocked the POTUS's mind (and yet all the signs are that this is not a man who readily questions his own certainties).

So, when you take into account both the speaker and what he is speaking about, you can only translate "You're in such good shape" as something like "Qu'est-ce que vous êtes bien conservée!" (You're so well preserved!) or "Mais vous êtes encore pas mal du tout!" (You're not bad looking at all for your age!) Shocking as it may seem, that is the only way to be faithful both to the explicit message and to the implicit content packed into what might have been a gushing compliment in his eyes, but which was in fact a deeply boorish and vulgar backhander.

So you need a thoroughgoing knowledge of the context to produce a good translation in general, and

1. "Look at that face. Would anyone vote for that? Can you imagine that, the face of our next president?" he said of Carly Fiorina, who was then in the running for the Republican ticket. Paul Solotaroff, "Trump Seriously: On the Trail With the GOP's Tough Guy," *Rolling Stone* (September 9, 2015).

a good translation of Trump in particular. But that's not all. You also have to *dare* translate him. Which is not always easy for people who find themselves having to translate him when it's not their job (like journalists, say), who may be perfectly capable of recreating simple declarations, texts, and extracts in their own language, but often fall short when the difficulty kicks up a gear, as is the case here. Again, the difficulty is not in the vocabulary or the syntax, but in translation's requirement for what is known in the jargon as "deverbalization," a way of disembodying the message so that it can be given a new form in a new language and a new cultural setting.[2]

Another example of the same problem: in one of those xenophobic outbursts that have become his specialty, Trump explained at an Oval Office briefing that he was *totally over* immigrants from "shithole countries." By which he meant various African nations, Haiti, and El Salvador. "Why are we having all these people from shithole countries come here?" he commented, adding that he would prefer the United States to welcome immigrants from countries like Norway.

While understanding the *meaning* of the comment was no problem for anyone, translations for "shithole" in the French media varied considerably. The January 12, 2018 edition of the daily newspaper *Libération* chose the expression "trou à rats," or "rat hole," for instance.[3] That seems a little weak compared to "pays de merde" (shitty countries) in *Le Monde*, "pays de chiotte" (countries down the crapper) in the Greek press (as reported by the French news agency AFP), and variations on a

---

2. I should point out that I am referring here to press & current affairs translation. There are a host of specialist fields in translation and the rules for translating news and political speeches do not necessarily hold true for other fields like technical, literary, or legal translation.

3. "Donald Trump: 'Pourquoi est-ce que toutes les personnes issues de trous à rat viennent ici?'," *Libération* (January 12, 2018).

theme of "paises de mierda" in the Spanish press. Daring to translate Trump is not as simple as the poverty & occasional vulgarity of his vocabulary might suggest.

For translators accustomed to translating the fluid, syntactically irreproachable speeches of his predecessor, Trumpspeak immediately proved to be dangerous territory. And this is deeply paradoxical, because when you read or listen to Trump, even if English is not your strong point, you feel like you understand everything. The vocabulary is ultra-basic, the sentences are short, even choppy, and the syntax…, how can I describe that? Well, it varies from day to day. Let's just say that in a traditional setting, such as a campaign speech or an interview, Trump's syntax alternates between extreme simplicity and total absurdity.

*

I'm not saying that there is only one way of translating a text, declaration, or political speech. There are many ways of saying the same thing and staying close to the original. But to create the same effect, it's important to take the context & the register of the language into account and stick to the rules for that kind of discourse. This is not a particular problem once you've been translating for a few years and have got into the habit.

When Trump first appeared on the international political landscape, the professionals responsible for translating him needed a moment to adjust. In line with his claim to be anti-system, he broke with all the previous political codes: with his election, America stepped into a whole new world in terms of society, morals, and communication. My own little niche of translation was likewise forced to adapt and find a new space to work in.

A Killer Interview

Like butchers and bakers ("It's slightly over, is that OK?"), teachers ("You've let me down, you've let yourself down, you've let the whole school down"), and actors accepting awards ("I love you mom"), in Western society, politicians give speeches that follow certain codes, or even clichés, in both form & content. They obey unspoken criteria, within the parameters of their own personality and political label.

What all politicians really want most of all is to be *heard*: as an instrument of persuasion, the form of their speeches is at least as important as the content. In the run-up to an election, they try to consolidate their party base and sway as many swing voters as they can. The idea being to create the best impression possible, they have to be polite and respect social mores — say hello to the lady, don't tell grandpa he has hyena breath, don't point and laugh at the poor and needy in public. For a politician, that translates into an unruffled, polite attitude and a similarly inoffensive register of speech. Being a good public speaker is crucial in creating a credible, professional image, though it can be a good idea to sometimes let the mask deliberately slip with a cleverly placed joke intended to make the speaker seem human.

When I was at translation school, one of the professors told us an anecdote to show us how important the interpreter's role is and why we must adapt to the register of the source language. In the 1980s, Georges Marchais, the general secretary of the French Communist Party, regularly traveled to the USSR to give speeches. Since he spoke no Russian, he was given an interpreter. The man spoke such polished, elegant Russian that Marchais earned a reputation as an excellent public speaker. Which was very, very far removed from reality and the picture anyone back in France got from his French.

I never could find out if the anecdote was true, but it left such an impression on me that it came back to me twenty years later, when I found myself having to translate Trump's speeches. Because the register the translator chooses for a speech already points to its overall content.

There are also tacit norms in terms of content, obeyed by most politicians. For instance, it is customary for newly elected American presidents to acknowledge their predecessor's merits, however briefly, during their investiture in Washington: "I thank President Bush for his service to our nation" (Obama, 2009), "I thank President Clinton for his service to our nation. And I thank Vice President Gore for a contest conducted with spirit and ended with grace" (George W. Bush, 2000), "On behalf of our nation, I salute my predecessor, President Bush, for his half-century of service to America" (Bill Clinton, 1993). No need to go back as far as John Adams to grasp that it is customary for the new president to thank his predecessor for his service to the nation before getting on with the important stuff. Trump didn't bother. He merely thanked Obama for his "gracious aid throughout this transition" — in other words, he thanked him on a personal level, despite refusing to read or even receive daily intelligence briefings throughout the transition period. Obama did warn him he would be "flying blind" if he didn't look at them. "We are grateful to President Obama and First Lady Michelle Obama for their gracious aid throughout this transition. They have been magnificent." And for the eight years of hard work before that, well, you can forget it. The same speech went even further, criticizing "a small group in our nation's Capital [which] has reaped the rewards of government while the people have borne the cost [...]. Their victories have not been your victories; their triumphs have not been your triumphs." What was that you said about the need for a conciliatory tone in the early days?

Trump nailed his colors to the mast from the outset. He would not bow to the rituals of the presidency.

Trump burst his way into well-mannered political discourse like an elephant in a china shop. Translators soon began tearing their hair out with his first speeches: on the level of both individual sentences and entire speeches, his language often seemed disjointed, sometimes even meaningless. It felt as if he were beginning a speech in his head and only began speaking half-way through the thought process. Which gave anyone listening (or translating) the impression of someone tossing words and ideas around in the air with no guiding thread. When you take an individual semantic unit or small group of words, some segments seem to mean something, but the general idea of the sentence is hard to grasp. The only recurrent element that Trump's audiences are bound to encounter, whatever the context, whatever the occasion, is ... Trump himself.

From a linguistic point of view, the first major shock came in late November 2016, when Trump granted the *New York Times* an interview, despite their turbulent relationship. This was the first official post-election interview, a few weeks before the inauguration. Naturally, it was hotly anticipated; Americans were now finally going to see and hear not Trump the presidential candidate, but Trump the president-elect, newly cloaked in the dignity of the highest office in the land. He would no longer need to be hostile or persuasive: the battle was won and the time had at last come to tackle the important questions.

Trump opened the interview by talking about his victory, the number of rallies he had attended daily, and the "very good" quality of the people he was about to appoint ("the quality of the people is very good," a bit like a pound of potatoes). He boasted about the rally attendance figures ("we had great numbers") and explained that he had never been a fan of the electoral college but now he was, for two reasons: "What it does do is it gets you out to see states that you'll never see otherwise." The second reason never came up (maybe because without the electoral college, he would have suffered a crushing defeat?). He added that he wished newspapers like the *New York Times* would be nicer to him ("I have great respect for *The Times*, and I'd like to turn it around. I think it would make the job I am doing much easier," which showed his very *unique* understanding of the role of the media and hinted at their future relationship). He then began taking questions from the journalists. And that was a step into a brand new linguistic dimension.

Between two Trump monologues on how much "the people" love him and the vast crowds at his rallies, Carolyn Ryan asked if his supporters would be disappointed if he didn't seek to hold Hillary Clinton to account. He said no, it was time to overcome "divisiveness" and "go in a different direction." And then he seemed to trip a fuse:

> Because our country's really in bad, big trouble. We have a lot of trouble. A lot of problems. And one of the big problems, I talk about, divisiveness. I think that a lot of people will appreciate ... I'm not doing it for that reason. I'm doing it because it's time to go in a different direction. There was a lot of pain, and I think that the people that supported me with such enthusiasm, where they will show up at 1 in the morning to hear a speech.
>
> It was actually Election Day, they showed up at, so that was essentially Election Day. Yeah, I think they'd understand very completely.[4]

Each individual segment of this quote is understandable. Yet taken as a whole and putting its clumsy syntax to one side for now, it is ... somewhat unclear, let's

4. "Donald Trump's *New York Times* Interview: Full Transcript," *The New York Times* (Nov. 23, 2016).

just say. If you use a traditional (I'm tempted to say "normal") translation technique to try and transmit the message in this quote, your brain will end up in a big knot. As is customary when a text is a bit too abstruse for its intended audience, the translator might be tempted to "contextualize" the translation by openly expanding on certain elements to make them simpler to read or discreetly developing an idea already present without altering or adding to the original message.

In this case, there can be no question of straightening things out to make the sentence easier to understand. It's not that it would be impossible to do so, because if you take a close look at the text you can more or less trace back the thread of the speaker's thoughts and understand what disjointed point he is trying to make; but smoothing out the contents would be so much work that you would end up with a declaration very different from the original. With Trump, the choppy format and apparently wild trains of thought are so much part of who he is that you find yourself forced to literally stick to the format of the original, or your translation will be unfaithful. Translators are used to dropping accidental repetitions and silently correcting occasionally errant syntax without changing the tenor of the message. But in Trump's case, improvements to syntax and form would be such a vast undertaking that it would not be translation, but a complete rewrite. The manner of speaking is just as important as the content of the message (if indeed there is a message in there), since it also reflects his character as a man and his thinking as a public speaker: so, such exaggeratedly clumsy speech forces the translator to do a good job translating someone who speaks badly, and therefore to write an awkward-reading translation. In truth, a translator who smoothed out Trump's syntax would miss the mark.

When you have spent the past twenty years of your career honing your language & thought to write clear translations, however demanding the speech, when you teach your translation students how to separate the wheat of style from the chaff and constantly require them to grasp the tiniest nuance of their mother tongue, that goes against the grain. Always stick to the message, never betray the author's thinking, and write a text that reads perfectly smoothly, a bit like Boileau's dictum: "What we conceive, with ease we can express."

And then, bang, in stomps Trump, wipes the slate clean, and forces us to revise our techniques for translating political speeches. It's not that the requirement for accuracy is any less, but rather that in his case, accuracy must be applied to the mediocrity of his style.

The *New York Times* interview was a fairly representative foretaste of Trump's later speeches and remarks. Choppy syntax, extremely basic vocabulary, and most noticeably the constant repetition of the same words — no fewer than 41 uses of "great," which seems to be Trump's favorite word, 25 "wins," seven uses of "tremendous," and the list goes on. As if Trump's mind were stuck in a loop, a closed circuit, on the scale of his vocabulary and hence his thought.

Not only does he repeat himself, but his vocabulary also goes round in circles in a restricted lexical field overflowing with superlatives. The most unsettling thing about this is that even if the words themselves are extremely basic, some of the first ones you learn to get by in English, they aren't always the easiest to translate. In fact, the most precise, scholarly, specialist words are less semantically ambiguous than words whose meanings are woolly or even empty.

Trump's unconventional approach to international relations has also shaken the strictly policed parameters of political communication, as for instance when he discussed Russia and ISIS in the same interview: "wouldn't it be nice if we actually got along with Russia, wouldn't it be nice if we went after ISIS together, which is, by the way, aside from being dangerous, it's very expensive, and ISIS shouldn't have been even allowed to form, and the people will stand up and give me a massive hand."[5] Or the Israeli-Palestinian conflict: "I've had a lot of, actually, great Israeli business people tell me, you can't do that, it's impossible. I disagree, I think you can make peace. I think people are tired now of being shot, killed."[6] Such infantile black-and-white thinking is at once a far cry from complex geo-political debate and light years away from the formulaic political blather that journalists (and translators) are accustomed to. Trump's unique relationship with the press has ushered in a new era for communication, where he alone holds the reins and there is no question of him molding the message to his audience and their expectations. Does he make no effort with his speech because he doesn't *want* to (he's the president! He can do whatever he likes!) or because he *can't*? Is he even aware that he falls below the average verbal skills of an educated adult, and especially of an American president? Is Trump alone in failing to grasp the change he himself embodies?

5. Ibid.
6. Ibid.

14

A Slap in the Face

Ever since Donald Trump was elected leader of the free world, it feels like I'm being slapped in the face on a daily basis. I don't think I'm alone in that. Given that that hasn't actually happened since I was a child, it's quite a shock to the system. Anyone who has ever been slapped knows that what really stings isn't the physical pain, sharp though it may be. No, it's the humiliation of being hit in the face, the defining feature of our humanity and personality, and the feeling of injustice that often goes with it. Because the ones doing the slapping are more powerful and know that they risk little in return. Slapping someone is a physical expression of an abuse of power. When the protagonists are more or less equally matched or the feeling of impunity less flagrant, they usually get straight to throwing punches and fighting. When you think about it, the first person to slap us in life is usually a parent or an older brother or sister — in other words, people in a position of authority.

With Trump, it's at least one slap in the face a day, whenever you open a newspaper / turn on the radio / check out Twitter. As a US president, he holds an absolutely dominant position — THE dominant position par excellence. And he knows it. The slaps come in all shapes and sizes, because Trump's psychological violence is constant and many-headed.

First and foremost, his violence is verbal. The words he chooses are uncommonly brutal. It's not just the semantic representation of warmongering, as when he wanted to unleash "fire and fury" against North Korea. Even his ordinary, workaday speech smacks English around. To start with, by repeating the same empty words — good, bad, great, incredible, tough, and the like — on a loop to refer to realities that we know to be more nuanced, he creates an impression of his own terrible use of language: and given

15

the hostility sometimes triggered by his supposed domination, that is something we could all do with-out. English is an extremely rich language (you'll have understood by now I'm not claiming to be objective here) that has developed over the centuries by borrow-ing from a whole bunch of other languages (particu-larly French: did you know, for instance, that English says pig, ox, and sheep for the living animal and pork, beef, and mutton for the cooked meat, because the latter were borrowed from French after the Norman Conquest nearly a millennium ago? The Normans took their own chefs along — I guess English cuisine already had a bad rep — and their vocabulary passed into the language). Being such a rich language, it has a host of evocative verbs, adjectives, and adverbs that stir the imagination. It's understandable that a non-native speaker might have trouble with them, nor would it matter much if your job didn't involve representing your country on the global stage. But a spokesman for an entire nation and its language with the vocabulary level of a fourth-grader is, frankly, painful for me to listen to as a professional linguist.

This stunted vocabulary, which I personally find excruciating, is not the worst feature of Trump's ver-bal violence. Yes, he butchers a language that has done nothing to hurt him. But when he says such frankly insane things as: "I would bomb the shit out of 'em. I would just bomb those suckers,"[7] his vulgarity per-petuates real violence. Just like he says women should be treated like shit or grabbed by the pussy.

Coming from a US president, this sort of lan-guage will make your eyes & ears bleed. At that level, couldn't it fairly be called verbal abuse? And what about the adjectives he chooses to describe an arms sale? In May 2017, the US president referred to a potential

7. Stated by Trump at a 2015 campaign rally in Fort Dodge, Iowa. See Rijin Sahakian, "What We Are Fighting For," *Open Democracy* (September 19, 2017).

arms deal with Qatar as "a lot of beautiful military equipment." When you know what the equipment is to be used for and what a controversial topic it is in the States, where firearms take thousands of lives every year, Trump's oxymoron verges on the obscene. The violence of his language, already clear when he was running for president, translates into political action: take the "Muslim ban" in the early days of his presidency — an attempt to ban citizens of seven Muslim-majority nations from entering the States — and his anti-immigration initiatives, including orders to separate hundreds of children from their parents at the Mexican border to "dissuade" would-be migrants. Trump's vocabulary makes no attempt to hide the fact that he sees Latino immigrants as vermin: in June 2018, he said he refused to watch them "infest" America to justify the cruelty of the measures against them.[8]

His actions accordingly give the impression he would gladly crush them beneath his heel, and here at least, you can't accuse him of not matching his words to his meaning. He speaks of migrants to the US as if they were more animal than human.

Then there is the daily flood of angry, vengeful, boastful, or absurd tweets from the presidential account, which it is almost impossible to escape without going to live in a cave with no internet. Another form of verbal violence exacerbating the impression of being swept up in a tornado of stupidity that threatens to stunt the thought processes of those subjected to it. How can you stop to analyze a declaration if, while you are thinking, the president has already vomited out another dozen? How can you dodge a slap when the person reaching for you seems to have as many arms as Medusa does snakes on her scalp?

8. From a tweet by Donald Trump. See Abigail Simon, "People Are Angry President Trump Used This Word to Describe Undocumented Immigrants," *Time* (June 19, 2018).

Well, Shit

Vulgarity isn't just about swearing. Shithole, grabbing women by the pussy, I'd date her if she wasn't my daughter, blood coming out of her wherever... Trump's vulgarity is constant, and we find it so shocking *because* it is totally out of place for an American president. Modern politicians are tacitly expected to act as role models, and most in fact do. This is one reason why politicians rarely let the mask slip, and when they do, the media and public opinion are instantly on their case.

When Nicolas Sarkozy blurted "casse-toi, pauvre con" (well fuck off then, loser) at a farmer who refused to shake his hand, the French media and public opinion were deeply shocked *because* it pushed him out of the presidential role he was expected to stick to throughout his time in office. It was the form that shocked people, not the content. He could perfectly well have said: "I have nothing to say to you, sir, now kindly move on," and no one would have batted an eyelid. It would never even have made the news.

What caused the media storm was his momentary, temper-driven lapse from the armor of politeness that he had to wear as an elected representative of the people. In both France and the US, as soon as the president is elected, he is no longer just a man: he is the embodiment of a role. By swearing on the Bible at the inauguration, the US president symbolically mothballs his own individual identity to become the voice and image of the nation. He represents the country at its grandest and most dignified, and as such it is difficult to forgive when he becomes the story, disrespecting his role and, consequently, the nation. Before Trump, the high water mark for vulgarity in international politics was Vladimir Putin boasting of his intention to "rub [Chechen extremists] out in the outhouse."[9]

9. See Michael Wines, "Why Putin Boils Over: Chechnya Is His Personal War," *The New York Times* (Nov. 13, 2002).

Vulgarity isn't just about how you talk, it's about who you *are*. One of the most revealing examples came during the campaign, when Trump began babbling incoherently, flopping his right hand like his wrist was broken, as if imitating the disabled journalist who questioned him about his groundless claim to have witnessed thousands of Arabs cheering as the Twin Towers came down. Then there was the October 2018 press conference where he told ABC News reporter Cecilia Vega: "I know you're not thinking. You never do." This vulgarity, verging on the insulting, diminishes his role as president and might seem counterproductive. Yet — and this is one of the great mysteries of the election — HE STILL WON.

*

Political correctness is a great bugbear of Trump's and he often prides himself on how un-PC he is. He even boasts of not being "presidential"; he declared in September 2018 that he had fallen "in love" with the North Korean dictator Kim Jong-Un who wrote him "beautiful letters," then grumbled, "But you know what? Now, they'll say 'Donald Trump said they fell in love, how horrible. How horrible is that? So un-presidential." He added, "It's so easy to be presidential. But instead of having 10,000 people outside trying to get into this packed arena, we'd have about 200 people standing there."[10] In other words, his blunt style is deliberate and his aim explicit: bums on seats.

Of course PC is a form of hypocrisy, a polite veneer that lets people smile to your face while possibly planning to stab you in the back. But it is also, and above all, a way of maintaining social harmony and kindness in our dealings with our fellow citizens. If PC means not saying what you are thinking, then it is sim-

10. See Michelle Mark, "'We fell in love … he wrote me beautiful letters,'" *Business Insider* (September 29, 2018).

ply the political version of the courtesy and respect for the rules that bind human societies together.

Think about school, for instance: no way could a teacher get away with telling a parent "your son is a bit of a dunce. He's a good kid, right, don't get me wrong, but Einstein he ain't." No, he will say: "Your son finds it hard to keep up in class, that's something we're going to have to work on, but I can say that he is one of the nicest kids in the room." The point is to frame the message as kindly as possible, using words to draw the sting so that the parents take the info on board without fainting clean away. It's exactly the same thought process behind explaining to our kids that they shouldn't shout out: "Look at that ugly lady!" or: "Look at that old man, is he dead?" I mean, yes, the lady might not be the most attractive, but it's kinder not to say these things. And if you really do have to say it for some purpose (which in Trump's case often seems open to question), then you wrap it up prettily.

Not Trump. He does not apply PC filters, the basic rules of social politeness applied to the highest political sphere. Apparently he is exempt, and he boasts about it as if it were an active choice. Actually, I'm inclined to think it's because he *can't* do anything else. He is incapable of filtering his thoughts because he can't adapt his behavior to suit the situation. This explains not only his extreme vulgarity but also his popularity with the margins of American society who feel that they have been taken for fools by a political elite that they cannot understand, and who see Trump's unguarded use of language, saying whatever comes to mind, as a stamp of frankness and honesty.

Liar, Liar

"Believe me."

On YouTube there is a brief video, 3 minutes and 23 seconds, posted by a certain vgolfoz. The title: "Donald Trump BELIEVE ME."[11] It is a montage of Trump at the podium saying "believe me" in a range of contexts. Armed with a ball-point pen and plenty of abnegation, I watched it on a loop to count them all: the editor manages to squash 76 different "believe me's" into a little over three minutes. And of course it is not an exhaustive list.

Interestingly, the video editor sometimes leaves in bits of sentences as context, creating moments of irresistible irony as when Trump says: "I have great respect for women, believe me"; or: "I am the least racist person you've ever met, believe me."

According to the *Washington Post*, which maintains an overtly hostile stance to the president — the feeling is wholly mutual — Trump told over two thousand lies in 2017. In 2007, the newspaper hired a fact-checker to check the truth of claims made by American politicians. He came up with the Pinocchio rating to measure the scale of a whopper. One Pinocchio is for deliberately hiding certain facts, partial truths, a degree of exaggeration or omission, but not outright untruths. The maximum, four Pinocchios, is for bold-faced lies. A topsy-turvy Pinocchio represents a flip-flop from a previously held position.

Since Trump was elected, the *Washington Post* fact checker has been working overtime. The newspaper gave the president four Pinocchios for his repeated claim that building a wall on the Mexican border would considerably reduce drug trafficking and abuse in America. This is wrong on two counts: first, most

11. https://youtu.be/Q3gFmielRS8

drugs come into the States either through commercial ports or secret tunnels and the wall won't help; second, the most abused drugs in the States are doctor-prescribed painkillers, and again the wall won't help.

In the notorious interview with the *New York Times* when he was president-elect, Trump justified his decision to hire Steve Bannon, editor-in-chief of the alt-right website *Breitbart*, arguing that Bannon was not the racist and anti-Semite he was often thought to be — far from it:

> Now, I'll tell you what, I know him very well.
> I will say this, and I will say this, if I thought
> that strongly, if I thought that he was doing
> anything, or had any ideas that were different
> than the ideas that you would think, I would
> ask him very politely to leave. But in the mean-
> time, I think he's been treated very unfairly.
> It's very interesting 'cause a lot of people are
> coming to his defense right now.[12]

Reince Priebus, soon to be appointed the White House chief of staff, added, "And what the president-elect is saying is 100 percent true."

Welcome to a world where simply *saying* something makes it true. One hundred percent true. Donald Trump, pants on fire?

It might be a bit more complicated than that. Are we sure these are lies? How can you judge if someone is in bad faith? Trump and his partisans and staff seem to be living in some sort of alternative reality. A world of "alternative facts," according to Kellyanne Conway, Trump's political counselor, on January 22, 2017. In their world, it's not about understanding, but *believing*, in the religious sense. At the September 26, 2018 press conference, a number of reporters questioned Trump

12. "Donald Trump's *New York Times* Interview: Full Transcript," *The New York Times*, op. cit.

about his Supreme Court nominee, Brett Kavanaugh, accused of sexual assault by several women. Did the president think the women were lying? Might Kavanaugh be guilty? "This is one of the highest quality people that I have ever met. And everybody that knows him says the same thing. And these are all false, to me" was his reply. In passing, the word "believe" crops up 21 times in Trump's responses at this press conference.

So he isn't necessarily *lying*. To be a liar, you need to be *aware* that you are distorting reality. What Trump is doing is telling his *own* truth, deeply rooted in his mind-world and disparaged by the people he accuses of spreading fake news. I don't think I could truly swear hand on heart that Trump is a liar, because he doubtless speaks with some kind of sincerity. When you are that far removed from reality, it's more like a form of denial that he can't really help, as he is just not lucid enough to be aware of it.

On the other hand, the people around him, his immediate entourage, the people who publicly back him — Pence, Conway, Mattis, and the like — seem far less likely to fall for Trump's false vision of reality. When his lawyer Rudy Giuliani served a stunned reporter the deeply Orwellian line "truth isn't truth" on NBC on August 19, 2018, he clearly tripped up on the lies dished out by the US administration, but not because he believed in them. No, he was just trying to justify his client's untruths in the Russia dossier.

The president's closest entourage is doubtless not persuaded by the parallel truth system built around Trump by Trump himself — to the point that one of the members of his administration felt the need to un-sully his reputation with an editorial in the *New York Times* in September 2018, justifying his stint at the White House while confiding that he and other leading figures in the administration had been colluding behind the scenes to neutralize the most dangerous and / or inept of Trump's decisions. Whatever their motivations (they say saving America: I say saving their skin from the inevitable blowback), it is clear that these people are not true believers in the president's fake reality: he is all alone in his bubble of insanity. Lies, like promises, are only binding if you pretend to believe in them.

Melania

I won't be writing a chapter about Melania Trump in this book. First of all because she isn't my subject, her husband is. It's not my style to criticize just because she married him and stays married to him, because I can't help but think (without the slightest shred of proof) that the reason she hasn't left one of the most hated men in the world is because he has found some way of forcing her to stay, or because she looks like a frozen-faced trophy wife just there to look pretty on her horrible husband's arm. It would be too subjective, verging on facial profiling.

Nor would I criticize her because I often feel pity for her, like the day she moved into the White House with her newly invested husband, when he left her behind in the car, totally ignoring her as if she were invisible. She had to go round the car alone to reach him and walk behind him up the steps without so much as a glance in his direction, to where the Obamas were waiting to greet them, showing the entire world just how little consideration her male chauvinist pig of a husband had for her. Even though the scene was the topic of much comment and comparison to the same scene eight years previously when the freshly elected Barack Obama graciously waited for his wife to get out of the car and ushered her to the steps before him, sharing with her his win before stepping through the doors of their new presidential home together.

Nor would I write about her because as a woman and a feminist, I am revolted by the idea that a woman should be allowed to experience motherhood on the sole condition that she snap back to a perfect body — and that she should agree. Nor because the repeated humiliation every time one of her husband's affairs comes to light makes me want to blame or pity her, depending on my mood that day. What other couples do is really none of my business. So who am I to judge?

And then this book is about language, and Melania Trump doesn't talk much. Especially compared to her blabbermouth husband. She rarely speaks in public and she has not said anything about the accusations of infidelity against her husband. Like the perfect First Lady, she attends charity events and has her photograph taken with sick kids, she hangs out with the wives of foreign dignitaries on official visits, but she rarely speaks. It must be said that when her husband won the Republican ticket, she faced a barrage of scorn when she claimed to have authored her own speech that just happened to plagiarize several passages from a speech by Michelle Obama at the 2008 Democratic convention: the real writer, Meredith McIver, eventually stepped up and admitted that she had indeed drawn on Michelle Obama's speech. Enough to pour cold water on whatever ambitions as a public speaker Mrs. Trump might once have held.

Melania Trump was born in Slovenia and only became a US citizen in 2006. Her English still has a slight Slovenian accent that is perfectly charming. Is that why she is so discreet? As the wife of a man who openly holds racist and xenophobic beliefs, who banned the citizens of a number of Muslim-majority countries from entering the States, who wants to build a wall on the border with Mexico to stop the Latinos he regularly insults from entering the country, who ordered migrant families to be split up at the border, is it not perhaps in her own interest to keep a low profile? Her status as a recent immigrant and the fact that her parents were only granted American citizenship *after* Trump became president seem so absurd, given his politics, that it would be perfectly understandable if she decided to stay in the shadows so that her husband was not accused of double standards in his private life and his policies for the nation.

I suppose I might be expected to comment on the infamous jacket Melania wore on a visit to a migrant child detention center. The back of the Zara jacket —

the affordable brand itself quite a surprise coming from the First Lady — was emblazoned with the slogan "I really don't care, do u?" at a time when the entire country seemed to be disgusted by Trump's decision to separate from their parents migrant children entering the country illegally, when people had been hearing and seeing footage of children torn screaming from their mothers' arms, feelings were running high and even the Republicans seemed to struggle to justify the move, let alone understand it.

I really don't care, do u? My first hypothesis is that the message was intended for critics of the policy to separate families, but why, then, wear it to a children's detention center? Pure cynicism? Happy-clappy, teach-the-world-to-sing types thought she might be sending a message to her Donald and was visiting the kids he was victimizing precisely to show him she didn't care what *he* thought. Her husband's explanation was very different and idiosyncratic: Melania was showing off her complete indifference to the media and her disdain for reporters. In that case, did he force her to wear it?

Did he really force Melania to wear a jacket *that cost less than fifty dollars?*

*

Unlike her husband, Melania Trump communicates by entirely non-verbal means. She communicates by her mere presence, and a number of clues indicate that she is often a reluctant attendee. Contrary to her husband, she sometimes gets the message across by subtle means that give the viewer a frisson of schadenfreude, such as when she stood stiffly and silently and refused to take her husband's hand as he desperately tried to grab her fingers while welcoming the Macrons to the White House in April 2018, or when she swatted his hand away in May 2017 on the red carpet at Tel Aviv airport.

Maybe because she used to be a model, Melania Trump communicates with her body and her image. Whatever she does will always be subjected to careful scrutiny and turned into GIFs. Having her photo taken at a press event in Michelle Obama's White House kitchen garden where she was supposed to be gardening with some wholesome American teens did her credibility some serious damage: dressed top to toe in the height of fashion, she didn't drop a single knee and seemed to be posing for a *Desperate Housewives*-style chic suburban garden catalog.

The woman is a mystery, her mode of communication is a far cry from verbal language, and I am not up to writing about her. I don't translate that mode of communication. And if every time she puts in an appearance alongside her husband or as the First Lady I get the impression that behind that perfect face she is inwardly screaming "get me out of here"; well, that's probably nothing more than a feminist fantasy and just my personal opinion.

Tweet, Tweet

Donald Trump is the first president to make Twitter the main presidential channel of communication. Twitter was born in 2006, and while Barack Obama did use it during his first election campaign, he has since said that he never wrote any of the messages himself.

Trump is a massive fan ("Twitter is a wonderful thing for me because I get the word out [...]. I might not be here talking to you right now as president if I did not have an honest way of getting the word out," he told Fox News on March 15, 2017), and it is where he pours out much of his verbal diarrhea. He seems to hop on it as soon as he wakes up and always has plenty to say about a whole range of topics. And if ever he runs out, he can always fall back on MAGA.

Twitter is an excellent way to study Trump's use of language. The now notorious "despite the constant negative press covfefe" (and since you ask, I decided *covfefe* would be a feminine noun in French), posted on May 31, 2017, demonstrates what an impulsive tweeter he is. Twitter is his dream mode of communication: its instantaneous messaging is used and read by millions of people. Its requirement for brevity is perfect for hammering home sound bites and slogans and short, choppy thoughts. Tom Roberts and Peter Oborne's book *How Trump Thinks* set out to draw up a Trump Twitter lexicon. They begin by explaining his use of punctuation:

'inverted commas'	— cynicism
?????	— incredulity
!!!!!!	— extreme incredulity
BLOCK CAPITALS	— anger

Next, they categorize words by frequency. For instance, the category "grabbing attention and signing off" includes three hundred occurrences of *"Wow!"* (the authors point out that the figures are rounded and all tweets are prior to April 2017, so they are more illustrative than mathematically reliable). In the same category, *"sad!"* occurs 250 times. "Praise — usually self-reflexive —" includes that firm favorite *"great"* and the superlative form *"greatest"* around 4,400 times. The other categories include "Written regrets," in which *"I regret," "I am sorry,"* and *"I apologize"* are slyly recorded at zero.

It's easy to point and laugh, but it's true that Twitter is the best way to communicate emotions as if they were facts. It's where people speak from the gut, spread rumors, share cheap clichés and empty platitudes stripped of their context. Trump can draw on his position of authority to pour out his own truths and responses, reacting to emotion and first impressions rather than thinking things through. He is far from alone in this: the Twittersphere often gets its panties in a bind but the debate is rarely deeply philosophical. The format does not lend itself to in-depth thinking: it suits superficial dialog and facile aphorisms. In Trump's case, it is a monologue that lets him justify his choices and his rants and to hammer home the propaganda message with short self-flattering videos and slogans in praise of him and his government. And of course, harangue the media in general and the press in particular, above all the *New York Times* and CNN — but not Fox News.

Here is an example from August 2, 2018:

> "Wow, @foxandfriends is blowing away the competition in the morning ratings. Morning Joe is a dead show with very few people watching and sadly, Fake News CNN is also doing poorly. Too much hate and inaccurately reported stories — too predictable!"

(The "Morning Joe" show on MSNBC had the day before debated accusations that Trump was obstructing Special Counsel Robert Mueller's inquiry into potential collusion between his campaign team and Russia. Fox & Friends is overtly pro-Trump.)

One of the problems of the digital realm is the feeling of impunity enjoyed by those who use it to cause harm. Nameless trolls, pests, and mudslingers feel empowered to vomit their bile behind the screen, confident that they will never be called to account since no one is there to witness them.

It's the same system for Trump: he spills out whatever crosses his mind, as if he were alone in the universe, nothing he says can blow back at him, and no one will ever check if what he says is true. Twitter is where he lets off steam, a kind of rough draft diary where he can toss out thoughts before thinking them through, while secretly basking in the knowledge that it will be read by an audience in the millions.

Twitter's brevity and reach encourages a kind of black-and-white thinking: good guys vs. bad guys. No need to back up your argument with sources or proof: on Twitter, Trump is past master of the old adage that you just have to look like you *know* you're right for people to believe you. The only downside is that on Twitter, no one ever changes their mind. His partisans see his laconic, peremptory tweets as confirmation of his politics and opinions; his detractors scoff and parade their outrage at what they see as his overweening pride and strings of garbled nonsense.

Take a tweet dated July 31, 2018 on suspicions of collusion between his campaign team and Russia prior to the election: "Collusion is not a crime, but that doesn't matter because there was No Collusion (except by Crooked Hillary and the Democrats)!"

Quite apart from the fact that it looks like he has come up with a new rock band (and now on 80s hits FM, Crooked Hillary and the Democrats!) for Trump, just saying on Twitter that there was no collusion is enough for it to be true. 240 characters is perfect for venomous little epithets like "crooked Hillary," "the failing New York Times," & "fake news media," drummed out relentlessly until the constant drip-drip-drip inevitably impinges on the subconscious of his followers. The historian Michael Beschloss has calculated that Trump's social media network extends to some hundred million people.[13] This reach is unprecedented in the history of the American presidency and the words poured daily into their ears (or rather eyes) cannot help but make their mark.

13. Tamara Keith, "President Trump's Description of What's 'Fake' Is Expanding," *NPR* (September 2, 2018).

Dystopia

One of my favorite films, Charlie Chaplin's 1940 masterpiece *The Great Dictator*, has often come up in relation to Trump's presidency. Chaplin's work of absolute genius features two characters, one a ridiculous tyrant of limited intellect with overweening ambitions, the other his double, a kindly little Jewish barber who ends up taking his place.

If you haven't already seen *The Great Dictator*, I would highly recommend it, first because it's a delightful film and a properly cathartic experience. When you see Hynkel playing with a big inflatable globe, on all fours on his desk bouncing it off his behind and bursting into tears when it pops, you can't help but picture Trump in his place. Or when you hear him barking into a microphone that cowers in terror at his invective, though the words themselves are indistinguishable. And then there's the premonitory title — *The* Great *Dictator.*

Of course, Trump might be racist and xenophobic, but he doesn't actually plan on genocide as far as we know. Far be it from me to compare him to Hitler, but rather to fictional characters based on Hitler. It is tempting to do the same with assorted tyrants from fictional dystopias written as warnings whose timeliness is now clear.

The book that has cropped up most frequently since Trump's election is George Orwell's *1984*, whose publisher, Penguin, hastily printed 75,000 new copies when Trump's advisor Kellyanne Conway first coined the phrase "alternative facts." She was justifying the Trump administration's claim that vast numbers of people attended the inauguration when the media images showed that in fact the crowds were rather thin. The significance of the expression escaped no one, and even the Merriam-Webster dictionary team felt the need to tweet the meaning of the word "fact":

"A fact is a piece of information presented as having objective reality."

1984 might not include the words "alternative
facts" *per se*, but there is a parallel to be drawn with
Orwell's newspeak and especially doublethink: "The
power of holding two contradictory beliefs in one's
mind simultaneously, and accepting both of them."[14]
This definition is nigh on identical to the "alternative
facts" touted by the Trump administration, which
imposes its own reality even when it flagrantly con-
tradicts demonstrable, fact-based reality, creating total
dissonance.

The theory was magnificently summed up by
Trump himself in July 2018 at a veterans' convention:
"Just remember, what you are seeing and what you are
reading is not what's happening." In other words, it is
only real when it comes out of my mouth (or that of
my close entourage), and anyone who tells you different is lying. Here, merely refuting what others have
said or done is not enough: only *he* can decide what is
real. This declaration was later reworded by Trump's
lawyer Rudy Giuliani: "It's somebody's version of the
truth [...]. Truth isn't truth."[15]

Kellyanne Conway, Donald Trump, and the members of his administration who constantly repeat untruths immediately torn apart by the media live in a
childish fantasy world where one just has to name reality for it to exist. "Let's play there were lots of people
at my inauguration." "Let's play it was the democrats
who decided to separate migrant children from their
parents." "Let's play climate change isn't real." It is a
kind of magical thinking, the belief that, if you wish
hard enough, it will happen, applied retroactively to

14. This quote and the quote at the end of the chapter are from
Orwell's *1984*.

15. Melissa Gomez, "Giuliani Says 'Truth Isn't Truth'...," *The New
York Times* (Aug. 19, 2018).

reshape reality. But who can read 1984 without a chill running down their spine? Who can fail to recognize that letting words transform the past is one of the key markers of authoritarian regimes?

"If the facts say otherwise then the facts must be changed. This way history is continuously rewritten."

Godwin's Law

Everyone thinks about it, everyone makes more or less veiled allusions to it, everyone tiptoes around the idea — but it's so tempting to draw analogies between Trump's xenophobic administration and the Third Reich and thereby fall foul of Godwin's Law, which states that as a discussion grows longer, the probability of a comparison involving Nazis or Hitler approaches.

Let me be perfectly clear: Trump is not Hitler, Melania is not Eva. The two situations are not comparable. The Weimar economy was catastrophic, times have changed, the cultures are light years apart, Trump is not a Nazi (though admittedly he did take a slightly disturbing length of time to wash his hands of the KKK after the racist violence that killed one protester & injured many others in Charlottesville in August 2017, and when he did it took him a laconic less than forty seconds couched in the most neutral, cliché-ridden terms: racism is bad, fine people on both sides).

Yet contemporary politics can only be analyzed through the lens of history, and this lens is so familiar, so thoroughly documented, that *not* mentioning it would verge on intellectual dishonesty. What's more, given the rise in populist parties across the Western world and the freeing up — and consequently normalization — of racist discourse in the media and political landscape, denying any similarity between the climate of hate in the 1930s and current developments would be an act of willful blindness.

In his essay "La Force de l'incohérence,"[16] Olivier Mannoni — a leading French translator who recently produced a new translation of *Mein Kampf*, a book he describes as "a monument of conceptual emptiness & aberrant syntax" — explains that "by breaking syntax

16. In *Contemporary French and Francophone Studies: Sites*, Vol. 21, Nº 5 (London: Routledge, 2017).

and rigor, the extreme simplification of discourse is the surest path to violence." Mannoni is an expert on Nazi Germany: he also translated volume three of Goebbel's diaries, describing him as a "frenetic scribbler" and the book itself as "alternating pompous sentences, exclamatory invocations, mangled sayings like 'clothes do not make a summer' and countless, endless adverbs." He also mentions Himmler, whose writing and speech features sentences that are "both simplistic and confused, an emphatic tone, repetitive style, and above all the use of almost childish words to refer to reality." Mannoni identifies elements in the SS chief's discourse that are familiar to anyone who has had to translate Trump: "Like the others, he talks about the 'bad world,' expressing a vision of the world where *schlecht* and *gut* [*bad* and *good* in German] are framed as basic, binary opposites, just like *bad* and *good* in Donald Trump's discourse." Eichmann, the architect of the Final Solution, sorted the world into good and bad people and demonstrated an inability to express complex thought. Mannoni explicitly compares Eichmann's rhetoric to the "fire and fury" Trump threatened to rain down on North Korea before it joined the list of America's allies. He explains that the binary language used by the "great men" of the Nazi dictatorship simplified thought and made it incoherent, and it was this incoherence that led to arbitrariness and authoritarianism. Without coherence of thought and language, there are no clear, precise rules to obey. Power can then indulge its whims and behave capriciously while the population is kept in constant fear of breaking rules it no longer understands.

One must-read for anyone interested in Nazi rhetoric and in how other totalitarian regimes use language is the book *LTI* — *Lingua Tertii Imperii: Notizbuch eines Philologen*, available in English as *The Language of the Third Reich*. It adds substance to the argument that Trump and his entourage's simplification of language and thought is a red flag. *LTI* was written by Victor

Klemperer, a Jewish-German philosopher who began studying how the Nazis used language in 1933. He kept a diary (in secret, of course) and when Hitler rose to power, he intuited that his atrocities — past and future — were facilitated by neutralizing the meaning of language and communication. Klemperer realized that language was a propaganda tool for the Third Reich killing machine and that it was able to be implemented quickly by imposing a particular type of vocabulary hijacked by the Nazis and retro-fitted with doctrinal content:

> The absolute authority exercised by the linguistic prescriptions of this tiny group, or rather of this one man [Gœbbels, the Minister for Propaganda], extended across the entirety of the German-speaking lands all the more thoroughly because the *LTI* did not draw a distinction between the spoken and the written language. Rather, everything was oration, had to be address, exhortation, invective.[17]

The lack of distinction between written and spoken language sounds eerily familiar when we listen to Trump's speeches and read his flood of tweets. Broadly speaking, in Trump's speeches on the campaign trail and now that he is president, what us translators have found most shocking is that for him, it is *all* about orality. He even writes like he talks; it's like he's physically there haranguing his readers with slogans and minatory tweets that often darkly threaten to accuse anyone who thinks differently of anti-patriotism. Trump lets rip, makes threats, swears his innocence, and makes accusations against his enemies, casting his dignity to the wind as in this tweet of July 25, 2018: "What kind of a lawyer would tape a client? So sad! Is this a first, never heard of it before? Why was the tape so abruptly

17. Victor Klemperer, *The Language of the Third Reich*, tr. by Martin Brady (London: Continuum / Bloomsbury, 2010) 19.

terminated (cut) while I was presumably saying positive things? I hear there are other clients and many reporters that are taped — can this be so? Too bad!"

He likewise uses Twitter to justify his ban on foreigners in black-and-white terms that, taken literally, verge on incitement to lynching: "Democrats want Open Borders and they want to abolish ICE, the brave men and women that are protecting our Country from some of the most vicious and dangerous people on earth! Sorry, we can't let that happen! Also, change the rules in the Senate and approve STRONG Border Security!"

I translated "some of the most vicious and dangerous people on earth" as "certaines personnes [i.e. individuals] les plus méchantes et dangereuses de la terre." This was the result of a deliberate decision to give Trump the benefit of the doubt, as I could have chosen to go with "certains *peuples* [i.e. populations] parmi les plus méchants et les plus dangereux de la terre," which would have extended the American president's wrath to entire nations. It is up the reader, based on their knowledge of Trump's character, to interpret his subtext.

Of course, Godwin's Law is to be avoided at all costs, but here we are dealing with a world leader who is casting aspersions on people who *already live* in his country in large numbers. He is talking about Mexicans and other Latin Americans who come to seek refuge in the United States, so this is not foreign policy propaganda as it might be in the case of North Korea or Iran — I doubt there are many North Koreans in America, given the hermetically sealed borders, and the Iranian community, coming from a country abhorred by Trump, is a small minority, and Iran was in fact one of the countries affected by the travel ban. It's one thing to publicly drag a population through the mud when they live on the other side of the planet, but it's quite another to call people the most vicious and dangerous on earth when they are members of a community that forms a large proportion of the American population and to tell Americans to look askance at the "othered" people living alongside them.

In the words of Victor Klemperer, "There is [...] a good deal of hysteria in the government's words and deeds. The hysteria of language should one day be studied as a phenomenon in itself."

*

"Endless repetition indeed appears to be one of the principal stylistic features of their language," Victor Klemperer was surprised to note in *LTI*, identifying that the slightest positive development was constantly held up by the Nazis, who automatically added it to their laurels even if it had nothing to do with them. Trump has the same linguistic reflex and the same endless mode of repetition: his thought process seems to be on a loop based on current events — both when speaking, as in his first interview with the *NYT* where he constantly harped on his election victory, and in his tweets, where he is capable of returning to the same topic to say the same thing several times a day. He is also a master of patting himself on the back for economic success stories that can only be the fruit of several years of work by the previous administration.

In imagining an America yielding to the siren call of authoritarianism, a further perturbing element is that Trump displays admiration and respect for world leaders who have largely been shunned by the international community for their dictatorial leanings. The go-to example of this phenomenon is the camaraderie (or even "love," in Trump's own words) between him and the North Korean dictator Kim Jong Un, but there's also his apparently sincere admiration and respect for the Philippines strongman Rodrigo Duterte, who stands accused of multiple human rights abuses — less widely known, perhaps, but equally disturbing. True, all presidents have to maintain relationships with authoritarian leaders, but Jamie Kirchick, foreign policy specialist at the Brookings Institution, has argued that: "What's different about Trump is that he often seems to genuinely admire these leaders […]. Trump is different because he ... likes the swagger, he likes the toughness, he likes the hostility towards the opposition and the media. And that's something new. We haven't really had a president who doesn't seem to express the concerns over human rights that his predecessors had."[18]

When Trump talks about dictators, he seems not to understand the significance of his own words. Take the time he told a rally in Raleigh, North Carolina, on July 5, 2016, that he'd prefer Saddam Hussein and Colonel Gaddafi to still be in power because at least they got things done — though admittedly he did concede that yes, "Saddam Hussein was a bad guy, right? He was a bad guy, really bad guy. But you know what he did well? He killed terrorists."

This bar-room banter takes on a threatening dimension when spoken by a man in the running for president, but Trump was good with that, and he still is. "I am a nationalist," he told one mid-term rally in October 2018. "Really, we're not supposed to use that word," he added, proving that he was indeed aware of its extremely potent political connotations. Trump openly prefers dictatorships to democracies when they serve his objectives. He was one of the first to congratulate newly elected Brazilian president Jair Bolsonaro, voted in on an authoritarian platform with shades of a return to military dictatorship. Is this a way of justifying the possibility of exceptional security measures suspending civil liberties, the equivalent of France's "state of emergency," depending on the whim of the leader and short-circuiting the democratic process and elected representatives?

18. "Trump's Latest Praise for Strongmen Includes Rodrigo Duterte, Vladimir Putin & Kim Jong Un," *ABC News* (November 14, 2017).

The nationalist paranoia that always goes hand in hand with dictatorial regimes is ever-present in the American president's words and deeds. Such regimes always justify their means by the necessity of defending themselves against a state-designated enemy, sometimes internal (enemies of the people), but more often external (immigrants). By sending no fewer than five thousand military personnel to the Mexican border in October 2018 in anticipation of a migrant caravan of just over four thousand Hondurans, described as "very dangerous" but which, it is worth noting in passing, had at that point only reached Mexico's southern border, over 2,000 miles away, and by promising to send between ten and fifteen thousand in total (in other words, more than three times the number of US soldiers in Iraq), and by announcing they would be authorized to use live ammunition on any migrants who threw stones at them, Trump established that the United States was under threat and that he was taking the necessary steps to protect its citizens. The message was hammered home by his administration when VP Mike Pence's press secretary Alyssa Farah described the group of migrants as "an affront to our sovereignty." The threat was entirely imaginary, but it was of a kind to convince not just Trump's own fan base, but a broad swathe of the American population vulnerable to clichés and prejudice.

Theoretically, America is not a dictatorship. But it might just be starting to sup with the devil.

Enemies of the People

Luckily, the checks & balances also fight with words. The press has always offered a significant alternative voice. Nowadays the media broadly speaking, encompassing radio, television, internet, and online press, is still a major counterweight in America, using language to challenge Trump and his "alternative facts." Of all of Trump's declared enemies, he is most virulently hostile to the media, particularly outlets that are not on his side:

> Freedom of the press also comes with a responsibility to report the news accurately. 90% of media coverage of my Administration is negative, despite the tremendously positive results we are achieving, it's no surprise that confidence in the media is at an all time low! I will not allow our great country to be sold out by anti-Trump haters in the dying newspaper industry. No matter how much they try to distract and cover it up, our country is making great progress under my leadership and I will never stop fighting for the American people! As an example, the failing *New York Times* and the *Amazon Washington Post* do nothing but write bad stories even on very positive achievements — and they will never change![19]

This lengthy four-tweet diatribe is brought to you by the forty-fifth president of the United States, who adds that the "media [are] driven insane by their Trump Derangement Syndrome," a disease invented by Trump supporters to attack the systematically negative reactions from his opponents to whatever he does. (The expression was inspired by the so-called

19. Donald Trump, July 29, 2018 tweets: https://twitter.com/
   realDonaldTrump/status/1023646663590797312

"Bush derangement syndrome," named by psychiatrist Charles Krauthammer in 2003 to describe "the acute onset of paranoia in otherwise normal people in reaction to the policies, the presidency — nay — the very existence of George W. Bush.")

There may be dozens (hundreds? thousands?) of other Trump tweets attacking the press, but this one is a pretty handy summary of the situation and his attitude to the media. Let's take a closer look:

— the blame game: "Freedom of the press also comes with a responsibility"... i.e. You are not doing your job properly and that makes you a bad person.

— "90% of media coverage of my Administration is negative." Let's quickly pluck a figure out of the air to bash the media — but numbers always look credible and can be used by those who go to bat for him. Numbers on Twitter very quickly get spread about and have their own little Twitter babies.

— "tremendously positive results we are achieving." Vague, no details about what results he has in mind, just take my word for it, OK? More of the same a bit later with "our country is making great progress under my leadership."

— "it's no surprise that confidence in the media is at an all time low." Another example of Trump's magical thinking. Saying it makes it true.

— "I will not allow our great country to be sold out by anti-Trump haters in the dying newspaper industry"... Oh, that's good. You can blame Trump for many things but you've got to hand it to him: he really knows how to use words to manipulate public opinion. First comes the flattery ("our great country"), making him irreproachably patriotic and anyone who disagrees with him anti-American (he does it again with

"I will never stop fighting for the American people!," unlike those media pinkos who are trying to tear the country down). Then comes the accusation ("sold out," which, let me note in passing, is exactly what he stands accused of in colluding with Russia. He has turned the accusation against his accusers, and again with "No matter how much they try to distract and cover it up," i.e. the same way he is trying to escape justice). The expression "dying newspaper industry" hints that it is bad (else it wouldn't be dying) and is a further example of magical thinking (if I say it, it is true — and the death of newspapers would suit the president just fine).

— Then come specific accusations against the *New York Times* and the *Washington Post*, which is owned by Jeff Bezos. Trump loathes the *Washington Post*, which awarded him three Pinocchios in 2015 for boasting that a book he published in 2000 predicted 9/11 and the war on terror. Ever since, the paper has printed scoop after scoop on how the 2016 campaign was hijacked and on possible collusion between Trump's team and the Russians. And he equally hates the *New York Times* which he claims only publishes negative pieces on him, which he calls "fake news."

— Finishing up with "they will never change!" is both an accusation of media bias by a man who sees himself as an innocent victim (see, whatever I do, they stick the knife in) and a condemnation. The newspapers are beyond hope, so who cares what happens to them — he won't lift a finger to save them and regularly pours oil on the flames. Take a little video that Trump's son Eric posted online, filmed at a Florida rally in July 2018. A crowd of Trump fans boo a CNN reporter for several minutes, chanting "CNN sucks! CNN sucks!" It is chilling to watch: the sight of an entire room full of people howling their hatred for a single man standing alone is a kind of symbolic lynching, and it's hard not to think that there's a fine line between symbols and acts.

I think it's important to compare this scene to what happened when Barack Obama spoke at a 2016 election rally for Hillary Clinton in Fayetteville, North Carolina. Mid-speech, the crowd began to boo a single, solitary Trump voter — an elderly gentleman with a chest full of what looked like military medals, waving a blue placard with red trim bearing the words "Trump" and "Make America Great Again."

A crowd of Democrats is no smarter than a crowd of Republicans, it must be said, and herd instinct soon had the whole room booing the heckler. Barack Obama immediately showed his annoyance. "First of all — hold up — we live in a country that respects free speech. Second of all, it looks like maybe he might have served in our military and we gotta respect that. Third of all, he was elderly and we gotta respect our elders. And fourth of all, don't boo. Vote."

The crowd calmed down, and the old man was escorted out, still brandishing his placard.

Trump accuses the media of being the enemies of the American people, using the language of propaganda reminiscent of twentieth-century European dictatorships, where the enemies of the people were always to be rooted out and destroyed. The expression was a favorite of Stalin's, who, you might recall, was not very nice to his political enemies. This is what the Khrushchev report "On the Cult of Personality & its Consequences" has to say about the matter:

> Stalin originated the concept enemy of the people. This term automatically rendered it unnecessary that the ideological errors of a man or men engaged in a controversy be proven;

this term made possible the usage of the most cruel repression, violating all norms of revolutionary legality, against anyone who in any way disagreed with Stalin, against those who were only suspected of hostile intent, against those who had bad reputations. This concept, enemy of the people, actually eliminated the possibility of any kind of ideological fight or the making of one's views known on this or that issue, even those of a practical character. [20]

In January 2018, senator Jeff Flake, an openly anti-Trump Republican who decided not to stand for the mid-terms to show his disapproval of Trump's policies, shared a similar opinion: "It is a testament to the condition of our democracy that our own president uses words infamously spoken by Joseph Stalin to describe his enemies."

Stalin did not coin the expression, which dates back to the French Revolution and was widely used by the Bolsheviks, but he certainly made it common parlance by using it to refer to those unfortunate enough to be scapegoated by the USSR. It is no coincidence that Trump — hardly a shining cultural beacon — picked up on the same expression. He may not be a great expert on Russian, or even American, history, but apparently he, or the advisor who told him to say it, knows how much of a punch it packs.

And it works. Trump voters howl down the press at his rallies and Trump shares the footage on his Instagram and Twitter accounts. He never misses a chance to criticize the press, gradually sowing the idea that you can't trust press criticism, because they're not just *his* enemies, they are enemies of the people, working

20. Nikita S. Khrushchev, "The Secret Speech — On the Cult of Personality," *Fordham University Modern History Sourcebook*, https://sourcebooks.fordham.edu/mod/1956khrushchev-secret1.asp, accessed August 19, 2020.

only to further their own nefarious ends. If Trump did ever manage to silence his media critics, then there would only be one version of events and the United States would find itself in a situation where political opponents would have to work in the shadows with a samizdat press.

I'm not saying Trump will get there — I don't think he will, because even though the media may be losing ground, it is still pretty powerful overall. America is not Russia or Saudi Arabia; reporters are not being killed by "accidents" or "stray bullets."

Yet, tempting though it may be to take Trump for a moron (and I am the first to hold my hand up here), it must be said that using manipulative language *works*. Constantly banging out the same accusations against the same people eventually shapes public attitudes. It hardly matters whether the manipulation is deliberate or not, whether the anti-press spin is purposely cooked up by secret cabals or not: the damage is done.

The two main newspapers targeted by Trump have countered his attacks with changes to their slogans. The *Washington Post* has chosen "Democracy dies in darkness," gently mocked by Dean Baquet, editor-in-chief of the *New York Times*, as "the next Batman movie." The *NYT* itself chose for the first time in seven years to take the truth as its theme in its Academy Awards ad, with the hard-hitting tagline "The truth is more important than ever."

I Read Areas

One of my kids is dyslexic. Dyslexia is a cognitive impairment that can affect individuals to various extents and has absolutely nothing to do with how clever you are. Someone with a touch of dyslexia might muddle certain words or find it hard to read fluently, but not necessarily struggle in their personal or professional lives. Someone with severe dyslexia, on the other hand, might never learn to read. It's not just about mixing up letters and reading Bs as Ps. I'm not a speech and language therapist or a neuropsychiatrist, but I do have a good layman's knowledge from having helped an *extremely* dyslexic child through school. This is what happens: when my child reads a text aloud — he can now, after several years of speech and language therapy — he identifies the letters and the sounds they make when they are put together. It is sometimes slow going, but he can do it. He can read. When he comes across an unfamiliar word, it's *really* slow going, but he knows he can do it, if he takes his time and has several goes at it. He is able to read an entire paragraph or even a whole page. He will, however, find it extremely difficult to explain what he has just read. Some of the words will have stuck in his memory and he will use his power of reason and background knowledge to put together a coherent meaning. Having expended all his cognitive energy on overcoming the reading challenge, he doesn't have enough left to tick the "understanding" box as well.

If you read him the whole page aloud, on the other hand, he will understand it all and will be able to give you a summary, no problem. Such severe dyslexia is like a partition in the brain. You can read, or you can understand. Not both at the same time. Just like you can't swallow your saliva and breathe in through your mouth at the same time, however excellent you are at breathing and swallowing.[21]

You can react in one of two ways to a diagnosis of severe dyslexia: you can accept it, or you can refuse to acknowledge it. If you accept it, you can begin to find coping strategies. Face the fact that your child will never read a book, and find other ways to give them that kind of cultural experience. My son reads with his ears. When he isn't asking one of us to read to him, he listens to audio books, now widely available in a range of formats with a host of classics and modern literature (you need tenacity: *Harry Potter* volume 5, for instance, is over thirty hours of listening). I show him films he decrees boring, I tell him stories about anything and everything — in short, I make his life hell by trying to open up his ears to everything I think he would have experienced with his eyes if he had "normal" access to books.

He has developed an extraordinary set of coping mechanisms in everyday life. He has an amazing sense of direction, he can put together furniture without reading the instructions (very serendipitous) and he could sell a drowning man a glass of water. He has an excellent aural memory. He makes up for his impairment in all sorts of ways. His short attention span (which often goes hand in hand with dyslexia) makes him impulsive, liable to dart from topic to topic and quickly lose interest in tasks that he has not chosen for himself. And of course he finds it very hard to concentrate (it goes with the territory).

People with this handicap (and it is a proper handicap) always find coping strategies. Particularly when they have not been diagnosed, have felt the need to hide their difficulties, and suffered as a result.

21. This is a case study, you understand. Depending on how severe the dyslexia is, some people do manage to read & understand simultaneously to some extent.

OK, you can see where I'm going with this. I'm by no means claiming to be expert enough either in this category of impairments or in Donald Trump's cognitive abilities. And as any specialist will tell you, you can't diagnose people at a distance, you have to see them, talk to them, test them. That said, I don't see why I shouldn't have fun with a bit of armchair psychology based on my own personal experience.

To excuse my impostor syndrome, I can point to no less an authority than the American Psychiatric Association which, in July 2017, sent its members an email lifting the "Goldwater Rule" banning them from diagnosing patients they had not personally examined. Mental health experts had been hotly debating the rule since Trump's election (though the American Psychiatric Association itself said it would be sticking to it). It is no coincidence that the controversy arose at that precise point in time: numerous mental health experts were wriggling in their chairs, arms waving, eager to shout out that the new president's behavior in public suggested an impairment or two that it might be worth looking into. When it comes down to it, what really matters is not whether it is possible, desirable, or ethical to debate the state of the American president's brain. Of course people can share their doubts and subject him to their armchair psychoanalysis or psychiatry. The salient point is that the debate arose at this point, and not under a different president.

But let's return to the issue. I'm no specialist in cognitive impairment, but I am positing that Trump not only has some form of attention deficit disorder (which would explain why he finds it hard to concentrate, goes off on tangents when speaking in public, tweets impulsively, etc.), but also that he *might* have some form of mild dyslexia.

It was a video that got me thinking. It was a deposition filmed in June 2016 about a lease agreement that was causing some legal trouble with the tenant.

The woman interviewing Trump, I guess the tenant's attorney, asks him how many leases like the one in front of him he has reviewed in his career.

"Signed, or reviewed?" he asks.

"Reviewed," she replies.

"Not too many. I signed hundreds. But I don't generally review them."

He goes on to explain that he leaves it up to other people — his employees or his children — to do the actual reviewing. He just signs them, eyes closed. OK, whatever. Let he who has never signed a new cellphone contract without reading all the fine print cast the first pen. The attorney asks him if he read the bit about damages. He says no. She asks him if he could read it now and tell her what he understands. (His own attorney objects — "Mr. Trump isn't a lawyer.")

"I mean, do you want me to read it? It's long. It's very long."

"It is long," concedes the attorney.

Then Trump turns the page & says, "I don't have my glasses on me. I am at a disadvantage because I didn't bring my glasses. This is such small writing."

He then says, "I can make it out. Do you want me to try?" And when the woman offers to have a larger print copy made and come back to it when he has his glasses, he says, "Let me just do it." He reads silently for a few moments, then attempts to sum up the relevant paragraphs based on a few key words he has spotted. "I mean, it's a complex clause, but it's a pretty standard damages clause, I think you will find."

Aside from the fact that it's pretty wild to forget your glasses when you're going to see your attorney, it seems clear to me that Trump used a range of strategies here to avoid reading the document in front of him. Since the first online whispers that the American president could not read, more and more evidence has piled up: for instance, he can be seen struggling to follow the hymn sheet at his inauguration, he has repeatedly trumpeted that he "doesn't believe in" teleprompters

52

and explained that he doesn't write his tweets, he dictates them. He has often said his favorite novel is *All Quiet on the Western Front*, but also that he doesn't have time to read. When Fox News anchor Megyn Kelly asked him about the last book he read, his reply was: "I read passages. I read areas. I'll read chapters. I don't have the time."

His ghostwriter, Tony Schwartz, who wrote *The Art of the Deal* for Trump in 1987, is blunt: "Trump didn't write a word of *The Art of the Deal* and I doubt he wrote a word of any of the other books that carry his name as an author," he told *The Independent*. "He doesn't read books and he doesn't write them."

Why doesn't he read? Officially, because he doesn't need to to reach the right decisions. He manages "with very little knowledge other than the knowledge I [already] had, plus the words 'common sense,' because I have a lot of common sense and a lot of business ability." Yet he says he loves reading. Asked by a Fox News reporter what he did to relax after a hard day at the office, he replied:

> Well, you know, I love to read. Actually, I'm looking at a book, I'm reading a book, I'm trying to get started. Every time I do about a half a page, I get a phone call that there's some emergency, this or that. But we're going to see the home of Andrew Jackson today in Tennessee and I'm reading a book on Andrew Jackson. I love to read. I don't get to read very much, Tucker, because I'm working very hard on lots of different things, including getting costs down. The costs of our country are out of control. But we have a lot of great things happening, we have a lot of tremendous things happening.[22]

22. Madeleine Sheehan Perkins, "Trump: 'I Love To Read,'" *Business Insider* (March 16, 2017).

The reason why Trump mentions an Andrew Jackson biography is probably because when he was running for president, he said he had no need to read any presidential biographies and he was told it didn't play well with voters. Marc Fisher, the *Washington Post* reporter he was speaking to, wrote in July 2016, when Trump was still a rank outsider, that "Trump's desk is piled high with magazines, nearly all of them with himself on their cover, and each morning, he reviews a pile of printouts of news articles about himself that his secretary delivers to his desk. But there are no shelves of books in his office, no computer on his desk."

Trump is open in his dislike of lengthy texts: "I like bullets or I like as little as possible," he told *Axios* in January 2017. "I don't need, you know, 200-page reports on something that can be handled on a page. That I can tell you." Though even bullets can trip you up, as he found to his cost in September 2017, when he read out a list of African countries he was thanking for official visits, one of which he misread as "Nambia" — capital "Covfefe," as numerous internet wags soon pointed out. What most people saw as evidence of Trump's disregard for Africa seemed to me rather to be a mistake by a hesitant reader who is finding it hard to read and understand a text at the same time. When someone with dyslexia encounters a new word, his brain simply cannot simultaneously read it, place it in context, and correct it if it is spelled wrong. Any other reader *without* a processing disorder would have corrected it — their *brain* would have corrected it — by the same mechanism that ptus the letetrs bakc in the right order if they get mixed up.

Yet one thing Trump does a lot is write. He is a frenetic tweeter. He has said in the past that he dictates part of his messages and relies, like everyone else, on spell check and voice recognition technology. The occasional mistake still slips through the net: in January 2015, he tweeted "We have enuf enemies."

There are plenty of examples of Trump's mistakes and avoidance tactics of the same kind, and it is fair to conclude that he dislikes reading, or if your mind works the same way as mine, that he finds reading hard, because he is dyslexic, or for whatever other reason.

And you know what? In the end, it hardly matters, because reading is by no means the only path to culture. In the 21st century, we have so many alternatives — audio-books, films, documentaries, internet! — that let us fill the gaps that might otherwise have been left by books. And not being able to read doesn't mean you can't think, or reflect, or learn, or seek self-improvement.

Big Head, Big Brain?

Trump is not a man of culture. His interests are business and golf. He has demonstrated a patchy grasp of his own country's history: "Even during tensions of the Cold War, when the world looked much different than it does today, the United States and Russia were able to maintain a strong dialog,"[23] he declared in July 2018, somehow overlooking the decades of more or less open conflict between the USA and the USSR — you know, little things like the missile crisis, the Berlin Wall, the Korean war... He also said that Andrew Jackson "was really angry that he saw what was happening with regard to the Civil War, he said, 'There's no reason for this'"[24] (mentioning Andrew Jackson again does rather suggest that it's the only historical reference he feels comfortable with and he's decided to crowbar it in wherever he can). He later set the record straight in a tweet: "President Andrew Jackson, who died 16 years before the Civil War started, saw it coming and was angry. Would never have let it happen!" This message was certainly intended to reassure his readers about his knowledge of history.

He's not great at geography either. "Belgium is a beautiful city," he told the crowd at a rally in Atlanta in June 2016. "Trump has an appalling ignorance of

23. "Remarks by President Trump..." in White House briefings, issued on July 16, 2018. See: https://whitehouse.gov/briefings-statements/remarks-president-trump-president-putin-russian-federation-joint-press-conference/

24. Which proves he must have had the best eyesight, since the Civil War broke out in 1861, sixteen years after his death. Not to mention that Jackson was himself a slave owner who sought to expel all Native Americans from the eastern United States and refused to speak out on the slavery issue, which hints at which side he would have chosen in a war that led to the abolition of slavery throughout the United States. But hey, I'm sure he was a great guy.

the current world, of history, of previous American engagement, of what former Presidents thought and did," Geoffrey Kemp, a former employee of the Pentagon under Gerald Ford and the National Security Council under Reagan, told the *New Yorker*.[25] Hence diplomatic gaffes such as telling Lebanese prime minister Saad Hariri on June 25, 2017 that "Lebanon is on the front lines in the fight against ISIS, Al Qaeda, and Hezbollah."[26] Hariri must have loved that, given that Hezbollah has been part of the Lebanese government for one quarter of a century (& when you're POTUS, you're kind of supposed to know this stuff). And Hezbollah was in fact fighting ISIS and Al Qaeda right then, as Trump was putting his foot in his mouth. He falsely accused Germany of owing the United States vast sums of money in NATO payments (actually, no one pays the United States NATO money). He said that North Korea was once part of China.[27]

On the economy: Trump's son-in-law organized a meeting with Goldman Sachs president Gary Cohn on November 30, 2016, to brief the president-elect on the major economic trends. Cohn was "astounded at Trump's lack of basic understanding"; he said that to avoid increasing the public deficit he would "just run the presses — print money."[28]

The problem with a president who is so ignorant is that decisions taken so lightly have far-reaching negative consequences for the country. The problem

25.   Robin Wright, "Why Is Donald Trump Still So Horribly Witless About the World," *The New Yorker* (August 4, 2017).

26.   Anne Gearan, *Chicago Tribune* (July 25, 2017).

27.   Just for the fun of it, let me tell you this little story. Stupidity is catching: the White House spelled the former British Prime Minister Theresa May's name wrong three times, leaving out the H. Not too bad, you might think. But Teresa May without an H is actually a porn star.

28.   Bob Woodward, *Fear: Trump in the White House* (New York: Simon & Schuster, 2018) 56.

is that his lack of general knowledge and his refusal (or inability) to read books, briefings, and reports, is the tree but for which you can't see the forest. There are plenty of ways of studying and learning without writing. We can train our aural memory to take over and live a perfectly normal life without reading. But you have to want to. And Trump has clearly shown that he does not want to learn. He thinks he already knows it all and can make his own decisions. The problem is not his stupidity — I'm actually not convinced he is all that stupid — it is his total and utter lack of intellectual curiosity. The problem is that when you don't embrace human culture, when you don't seek out other people's experiences, you can't access the level of thought sparked by exposure to culture, even if you're unaware of it. Trumpspeak is stuck in a loop, like his speeches, his thought patterns, and his political stance, as he doesn't listen to anyone else when making decisions. Another downside to refusing to learn is that hearing about other people's experiences is what triggers empathy. You have to experience a range of points of view to step out of your own skin and adapt your thinking to other, unfamiliar patterns.

In refusing to learn, Trump is refusing to open up to the possibility of empathy. That might explain why he cannot reach beyond clichés when faced with an emotionally demanding event such as the death of a public figure or a mass shooting. The refusal to learn can be read two ways: as the result of his stubborn personality, or of a deep-rooted fear of revealing his weaknesses. No one likes to be exposed and it's hard to admit that you don't know something that is held to be common knowledge.

In this case, Trump has found a way of masking his ignorance. When he learns something new (I mean let's not be reductive, it does happen!) he doesn't say, "Hey, listen up, I've just learned something!" He turns the situation around, trumpeting that no one knows this great fact that he's about to share with you.

It usually starts something like: "Nobody knows…" or: "People don't know this…"

"Abraham Lincoln. […] Most people don't even know he was a Republican. Right? Does anyone know? A lot of people don't know that," he said at a fund-raising dinner in March 2017. Given that he was talking to a room full of Republicans, and that the party likes to call itself the party of Lincoln, yes, there's a fair chance that some of them knew. This speech put me in mind of those show-offs who like to regale their audience with little snippets they've just learned (I do it all the time myself — did you know the poet Verlaine's mother kept her own miscarried fetuses in formaldehyde?). Then there's this little gem: "Nobody knew that health care could be so complicated." Again, well, yes, a lot of people did have some inkling of that, even non-specialists. But Trump only found out after his election, when he set out to overturn Obamacare.

"France is America's first and oldest ally. A lot of people don't know that," he told President Macron in Paris in July 2017. People across France thanked him for drawing this little-known fact to their attention. And here's a quote from a speech on April 5, 2018 on China's threat to world trade — I love this one, it's so ironic — "We have our intellectual property, and a lot of people don't understand what that means."[29]

And who knew foreign policy is such a complicated business? Trump told the *Wall Street Journal* (April 12, 2017) that he learned in his first interview with Chinese president Xi Jinping that China could not step in and solve the North Korea nuclear problem: "After listening for ten minutes, I realized it's not so easy. I felt pretty strongly that they had a tremendous power over North Korea. But it's not what you would think." Well, my word, who knew?

29. Jenna Johnson, "'People Don't Realize': Trump & the Historical Facts He Wants You To Know," *Washington Post* (April 18, 2018).

One last example: Brexit. "It's a very complex problem, I think nobody had any idea how complex that was going to be…. Everyone thought it was going to be: 'Oh, it's simple, we join or don't join, or let's see what happens,'" he told the British journalist Piers Morgan on his return from a visit to Britain.

How did a man so proud of his own ignorance manage to get elected to the White House? Is it fair to speculate that might be partly *why* he won? Since his election, Trump has maintained a faithful voter base who see him as the embodiment of a simpler, humbler America, the average hard-working Joe who risks losing his job to the villains *du jour* — Indian, Chinese, Mexican. The America of the rust belt and the corn belt, struggling with economic decline. This America could care less for the East Coast intellectuals who look down on them from their comfortable diploma-lined studies and preach down to them while nibbling on organic gluten-free tofu burgers in vegan restaurants.

So answer me this: which Americans were the most hopping mad about Trump's election, and above all why? According to his opponents (and much of the rest of Western society), the former reality TV star's decisions in matters human, economic, and scientific run counter to common sense. People are *so* up in arms because on the one hand he represents a brand of far-right politics that they despise, and on the other he is an ignorant, junk-food-and-soda-addled fool, who can't talk properly, barely reads, and only ever speaks about money. In short, he is what we call in French a *beauf.* Joe Sixpack writ large. In the words of Yale historian David W. Blight, "As for historical analogies and understanding, our President seems incapable of even getting something wrong in reasonable or interesting ways."[30]

30. http://www.davidwblight.com/public-history/2017/8/25/
trump-and-history-ignorance-and-denial-national-under
ground-railroad-freedom-center, link accessed on 8/26/2020.

Lefties are fuming because Trump pours scorn on culture and *gets away with it*. All the debates, articles, and cries of indignation against the American president come from brains horrified that you can be (or at least come across) as stupid as a donkey and *still* be that outrageously successful. Each one of Trump's words is the absolute negation of the Enlightenment embraced by entire swathes of American society. And even harder to swallow is the fact that whatever the lefties do — wring their hands, stamp their feet, write pointed articles on Trump's unfitness for office and the hopelessness of his team — nothing stops him, and it all bounces off his thick hide.

For left-leaning Americans, Trump's election was not just a political disaster, it was a major societal defeat. "America's Golden Age of Stupidity," the *Washington Post* headlined a July 25, 2017 article by David Rothkopf: "The opposite of knowledge is ignorance. But the willful disregard of knowledge — regardless of motive — is stupidity."

But let's stand on the other side of the divide for a moment. Trump's election is a victory for white trash, the left-behinds, the forgotten fringes of American society. Trump has managed to convince them he is one of them — forget his luxury towers around the world, his ostentatious displays of wealth, his love of bling, the platinum spoon in his mouth from birth. He is rich, but he's the man the white trash aspire to be, given the chance. He talks like them, he shoots straight from the hip, and he speaks their language. What delicious revenge against the lefties who are so sure they are the intellectual elite, who crush the average blue-collar guys with their culture and their sophisticated thinking. Yes, Trump's overt stupidity, his message that you just have to want something for it to happen, his unabashedly simplistic thinking, appeal to a whole swathe of the population that has long been impotently seething. Trump's people do not read the *New York*

Times or the *Washington Post.* They live far from the East and West coast — a lot of them are in the deep South — and they, at long last, have a president who shows he knows them. Who *listens* to them.

Tilting at Windmills

Early in his presidency, Barack Obama told the *Washington Post* that decisions had to be taken on the basis of information, not emotion. This turned out to be the exact opposite of Trump's tactic. His approach is to follow his instincts and hold a finger up to see which way the wind is blowing. He does not trust experts as a matter of principle. When *Morning Joe* (MSNBC) in the spring of 2016 asked Trump about foreign policy advisers, his response was: "You won't like the answer, but the answer is me. I talk to myself."

Trump also trusts himself a great deal when it comes to science. The White House has its own team of scientific advisors — nine people in Obama's day. The numbers gradually thinned out after Trump's arrival and his administration has free-wheeled many, many decisions on science issues. Not until August 2018, more than a year-and-a-half after he became president, did he appoint a scientific adviser. This means he began negotiations on North Korea's nuclear weapons program and withdrew from the Paris Agreement on climate change without expert scientific advice.

Trump thinks climate and weather are the same thing, so whenever it snows in New York, he takes it as proof that climate change is a hoax. In 2012, he tweeted that: "Global warming has been proven to be a canard repeatedly over and over again" [sic]. On November 6 of that same year, he informed his followers that: "The concept of global warming was created by and for the Chinese in order to make US manufacturing non-competitive." (Nope. Not a clue here what he was on about.) He returned to the subject in a December 16, 2013 tweet: "Ice storm rolls from Texas to Tennessee — I'm in Los Angeles and it's freezing. Global warming is a total, and very expensive, hoax!"

At least Trump has been consistent on this point: since he became president, he has reduced the Environmental Protection Agency budget and appointed as its administrator Scott Pruitt, a former oil industry lobbyist and a climate change skeptic. Pruitt eventually resigned after a number of financial scandals and thirteen federal investigations with him on the sharp end. He was a firm believer that climate change was not man-made. Trump then appointed one of his most faithful supporters, Andrew Wheeler — a less flashy figure — who also found it hard to believe that climate change was anthropic in origin. "The fact is that the climate changes regularly," he told a reporter in 2006, chiming in perfectly with his new boss's views. For the record, it is only fair to say he has watered down his views some since his appointment: "I believe man has an impact on the climate but what is not completely understood is what the impact is."[31]

Trump logically decided to pull America out of the Paris Agreement on climate change, whose signatories undertook to introduce measures to reduce greenhouse gas emissions and try to get a grip on rising temperatures. He then followed up by signing a decree on energy independence that killed off Obama's Clean Power Plan with its strategy to develop renewable energy sources. Trump is a big fan of coal. "[America has] more than 250 years worth of beautiful clean coal," he boasted in August 2017, and again in January 2018 in his State of the Union address: "we have ended the war on beautiful, clean coal."

Trump, not a man to shy away from oxymorons, loves "clean coal" as much as he hates killer wind turbines. For him, the greatest quality of coal — aside from the fact that America is full of it and it lets him create new jobs in an industry decimated by technological advances, growing awareness of green issues, and above all his much loathed predecessor — is one that comes particularly high up on his own narcissistic

31. Ellen Knickmeyer, "EPA's New Boss Unlikely To Change Trump Environmental Policy," *AP News* (July 7, 2018).

scale: it is *indestructible*. And he proves it: "We love clean, beautiful West Virginia coal. And you know, that's indestructible stuff. In times of war, in times of conflict, you can blow up those windmills, they fall down real quick. You can blow up pipelines, they go like this. You can do a lot of things to those solar panels, but you know what you can't hurt? Coal. You can do whatever you want to coal. Very important."[32] It's arrant nonsense, of course, but that's another story. What's interesting is that he believes it, and that he puts it in those terms.

Trump's black-and-white use of language (and hence, one can safely deduce, thinking) is particularly flagrant when it comes to energy policy. Coal: good. Clean. Beautiful. And bad, you ask? Bad is wind turbines. Yes, really. Trump has argued on several occasions that wind turbines kill birds, and that's good grounds to be against them. (Did I say he was short on empathy? I take it back.) In 2016, he got all steamed up about it on the radio: "[Wind power] kills all the birds. Thousands of birds are lying on the ground. And the eagle. You know, certain parts of California — they've killed so many eagles. You know, they put you in jail if you kill an eagle. And yet these windmills [kill] them by the hundreds." He returned to the question in August 2018: "They kill the birds. You want to see a bird graveyard? You just go. Take a look. A bird graveyard. Go under a windmill someday."[33] But hope is not lost! Because in the same speech, Trump also claimed that wind turbines (or windmills, as he called them) are extremely vulnerable and therefore unreliable: "You can blow up the windmills. You know, the windmills. Boom, boom, boom. Bing. That's the end of that one.

32. Linda Qiu, John Schwartz, "Trump's False Claims About Coal, the Environment, & West Virginia," *The New York Times* (Aug. 21, 2018).

33. Ros Davidson, "Rollback On Energy's Bird Kills Reveals Trump's Wind Hypocrisy," *Windpower Monthly* (February 28, 2020).

If the birds don't kill it first. The birds could kill it first."[34] In Trump's mind, birds *can kill wind turbines*, in some kind of Hitchcock revenge drama, I guess, though the finer details escape me.[35]

In conclusion, "coal is doing great" because coal is not a sissy like those windmills, which can be knocked down with a feather. Yet according to the American administration's own analyses, the new coal regulations could cause up to 14,000 premature deaths a year by 2030 as rising levels of particles trigger more heart and lung disease. Trump clearly hasn't read Cervantes, but he certainly has seen one or two Hitchcock films and mistaken them for documentaries.

Climate change is not a reality in Trump's world. Or rather, it's a reality that depends upon America's economic interests as he sees them. It's a *relative* reality. When he gave the *NYT* that killer interview, one of the reporters asked him, "Do you think human activity is or isn't connected [to climate change]?" His response: "I think right now ... well, I think there is some connectivity. There is some, something. It depends on how much. It also depends on how much it's going to cost our companies. You have to understand, our companies are noncompetitive right now."

Since Trump had got it into his head that coal was going to save the American economy, yet he cannot *not* know that coal is a highly pollutant form of energy that has greatly contributed to climate change, he simply decided to solve the equation by blanking out one of its halves. Unlike "traditional" politicians,

34. Extracts from a speech by Donald Trump at a fund-raising dinner on August 20, 2018.

35. Let me point out here that Trump's administration allowed Americans to bring back hunting trophies from Africa and lifted the ban on hunting hibernating species like wolves and polar bears in Alaska, probably because in the absence of natural predators like wind turbines, they might proliferate to a dangerous extent.

he's not the kind to skirt round the issue. He just says "climate change doesn't exist," and boom, no more climate change. He says coal is clean — problem solved. And this is where we tip over into a situation straight out of *1984*: in the fall of 2017, the EPA began scrubbing references to climate change from its website, in the grand tradition of totalitarian governments: if you don't talk about it, it doesn't exist. The EPA website also took down its pages outlining the risks of climate change and the approaches various nations were taking to combat it. As of the time of writing,[36] the climate change glossary link on the EPA website takes you to a page that says it is being "updated."

36. Translator's note: this refers to the French original.

Funnyman

Trump certainly has a sense of humor. He has shown it off in the course of his dozens, maybe hundreds, of public appearances. When the radio host Hugh Hewitt reminded him he had promised to share his tax return on his program, Trump replied, "First of all, very few people listen to your radio show, that's the good news." Then there was the time at a campaign rally when a baby started crying and he told the mother, "I love babies. I love babies. I hear that baby crying — I like it. What a baby, what a beautiful baby. Don't worry, don't worry. The mom's running around, like don't worry about it, you know. It's young and beautiful and healthy and that's what we want" — a pretty unexpected display of empathy. But the baby would not stop, and a few beats later Trump stopped talking in the middle of a sentence to tell her, "Actually, I was only kidding — you can get that baby out of here [...]. I think she really believed me that I love having a baby crying while I'm speaking."[37] It was mean, but it was also kinda funny (except for the poor mom, of course).

Another example that comes up online when you Google "Trump" and "funny": during a Fox News debate, anchor Megyn Kelly reminded Trump that: "You've called women you don't like 'fat pigs,' 'dogs,' 'slobs,' and 'disgusting animals.' Your Twitter account —." Trump interrupted her with a smile: "Only Rosie O'Donnell!"[38]

Then there was the time Trump openly mocked the testimony of Christine Blasey Ford, the academic who accused Trump's Supreme Court nominee Brett

---

37. Ashley Killough, "Trump: 'You Can Get the Baby Out of Here,'" *CNN* (August 3, 2016).

38. He also said Rosie O'Donnell talks like a truck driver. I'll give you one guess why.

Kavanaugh of sexual assault, imitating her to the point of ridicule, to whoops and cheers from the crowd. He *is* a pretty good mimic, it has to be said.

All these displays of wit have something in common. They are all instances of one particular type of humor, based on aggression. Rod Martin, professor of psychology at the University of Western Ontario, is an expert on humor and well-being. He has defined four categories of humor: affiliative (which helps develop social bonds), self-enhancing, self-defeating, and aggressive. While we all use all four types to varying degrees depending upon the circumstances, we have one dominant type. Rod Martin considers that the latter two reflect a degree of maladjustment — particularly the aggressive humor often wielded by Trump, going on the attack to trigger a laugh. We all know someone who is an expert in serving up burns, bringing their victims to the verge of tears or making them lash out, and then saying "C'mon man, can't you take a joke? Where's your sense of humor?"

René Proyer, professor of clinical psychology at the University of Zürich, has written that a systematic preference for this kind of humor is typical of people with anti-social behavior who are impulsive, egocentric, and lacking in remorse. "The limit is when you deliberately accept hurting people to be funny. That's no longer friends sharing a laugh, but a strategy to assert your dominance and crush other people."[39]

When Trump cracks a joke, it's always easy to understand and translate: you can always take it at face value, and when there are layers of meaning, they are so transparent that they don't take much thought to peel back. Whether deliberate or forced, this kind of humor is not what you might call subtle.

There's another kind of joke Trump tells when he's not trying to take out a rival or a critic: he likes to

39. "Le rire mauvais: quand l'humour devient nuisible," *Le Monde de l'intelligence* (30 April–May 2013).

puff himself up and hog the conversational limelight. Back to that killer *NYT* interview again: one of the reporters asked him about climate change — a matter of personal interest, surely, as he owned a number of golf courses along the coast — he joked that climate change would be great for some of them, like Doral, which was a bit far inland at the moment.

Obama's former speech-writer David Litt penned an article in the *New York Times* in September 2017 about how uncomfortable Trump's humor made him. He wrote that Trump only seemed capable of making jokes to the detriment of other people, and also pointed out something that made him very ill-at-ease: Trump *never laughs*. Litt wrote about looking long and hard and finding just one case of the president actually laughing. That was when a dog started barking at a rally, and someone in the crowd shouted "It's Hillary!" Trump burst out laughing.

Trump is also the first president since Ronald Reagan in 1981 to skip the White House Correspondents' Dinner, a major annual event where the president is supposed to make a witty speech nailing everyone in the room.[40] Obama did a particularly great job. While it seems pretty obvious that Trump's permanent state of hostility toward the press was the main reason, it also seems likely that it would be a big reach for him — partly because he would have to *read* a speech full of jokes and not be able to go off-piste (and we all know how reluctant he is to read), but also because being funny means constantly keeping on just the right side of decency and teasing, without overstepping the line. Trump is not a complete idiot: he knows perfectly that this is not his strong game. There's nothing worse than telling jokes that fall flat. Especially when you

---

40. And Reagan had a really good excuse: he'd just been shot. When he was whisked into the operating theater, before he was put under, he looked at the surgeons and said: "Please tell me you're Republicans."

know the audience will be only too pleased to help your failure go viral.[41]

Then there are all the times that Trump was funny without meaning to be. Like when he calls himself a genius. Or says he has great respect for women. Or when he said: "Part of the beauty of me is that I'm very rich."[42] Or when he said that Hurricane Florence, which hit the Carolinas in September 2018, was "tremendously big and tremendously wet, tremendous amounts of water," helpfully adding that it was "one of the wettest the US has ever seen from the standpoint of water."[43] My personal favorite is his explanation of the weather at his inauguration: it was threatening rain until God stepped in and said no, that wouldn't be nice: "It was almost raining [...]. But God looked down and he said we're not going to let it rain on your speech."[44]

41. Another reason why Trump might be so hostile to the correspondents' dinner is that in 2011, in response to Trump's birther nonsense, Obama triumphantly skewered him in front of the entire room. The story goes it was this humiliation that made Trump decide to run for president.

42. Bess Levin, "Trump 'The Beauty of Me'...," *Vanity Fair* (October 8, 2018).

43. Karma Allen, "Trump skewered after calling Hurricane Florence 'tremendously big and tremendously wet'," *ABC News* (September 12, 2018).

44. Politico Staff, "Trump, Pence Remarks at CIA Headquarters," *Politico* (January 21, 2017).

What About God?

Trump has a very special relationship with God. Like most Americans, you might think. For us French, wedded to the separation of church and state, the idea of having God on your money, in your courtrooms, and constantly cropping up in political speeches is pretty weird. Like almost every president before him, Trump swore allegiance on the Bible — in fact on two, his own and the one used by an earlier leading Republican, Abraham Lincoln (Obama chose the same one in 2008, fact fans). While presidents do have to swear the oath of office at their inauguration, nothing in the American constitution says it has to be on a Bible. That particular fashion was started by George Washington back in the day. In 1825, John Quincy Adams became the first to swear on a book of law (he was also the first to do so in long trousers rather than breeches. Quite the trend setter). In 1901, Theodore Roosevelt was sworn in hastily after President McKinley was assassinated and no one could lay their hands on a Bible for the ceremony, which lasted ten minutes at most and was held at a friend's house. Likewise, after Kennedy was shot, Lyndon B. Johnson swore the oath on board Air Force One on a Catholic prayer book found in a bedside table.

Trump bowed to tradition, but it was a last-minute thing. According to Omarosa Manigault Newman, a White House director of communications before she was fired and published a tell-all book on Trump, his original plan was to use a very different book for the oath: his very own *Art of the Deal*. "It's the greatest business book of all time," Trump said, according to Omarosa. "It's how I'm going to make great deals for the country. Just think how many copies I'd sell — maybe a commemorative inauguration copy?"

Just joking, folks.

So God showed his gratitude that Trump decided in the end to go with *his* best-seller for the inauguration by holding off the rain.

Trump clearly has some kind of relationship with God, but what exact form it takes is something of a mystery. God is on Trump's side, naturally, but I do sometimes wonder if Trump doesn't mistake himself for the big guy. His megalomania, his obvious delight in power, and the qualities he sees in himself seem to make him a God-like figure.

His tendency to rely on belief over science, the fact that he creates his own reality, an "alternative" world that obeys his rules, the way he just has to say something for it to to be true, his conviction that he knows more about everything than everyone else without actually having to learn it ("I know more about ISIS than the generals do," he claimed in October 2016), all suggest that his megalomaniac leanings are verging on a claim to divinity. "Nobody loves the Bible more than I do," he told one campaign rally. Nobody "builds better walls," nobody "understands the horror of nuclear" more than him. And there's plenty more where those came from.

If you have a minute, hop on to YouTube and watch the first public prayer meeting in the Oval Office on September 1, 2017, after Hurricane Harvey. You will see Trump sitting at his desk, eyes downcast, hands joined in humble prayer (no, really), surrounded by a group of pastors reaching over to touch his shoulders, like disciples round the Messiah. One of them prays for several minutes, thanking the Lord above for making Trump president.

At the May 2018 National Day of Prayer (introduced by Congress in 1952), Trump pointed out that since he had taken office, the expression "under God" had been much more widely used (the religious reference was added to the pledge of allegiance to the American flag in 1954 to reaffirm "the transcendence of religious faith in America's heritage and future; in this way we shall constantly strengthen those spiritual weapons which forever will be our country's most powerful resource, in peace or in war.") In other words, God is on our side, not like those dirty Commies.

He also takes credit for the fact that Americans are now happy to say "Merry Christmas": "We're starting to say Merry Christmas again …. You notice a big difference between now and two or three years ago?" When he makes claims like this, he is positioning himself as the Lord's mouthpiece, His spokesman on earth, strengthening his stance on issues such as the pro-life movement. "Nothing is more powerful than God," he said the same day, just in case someone didn't get the (Christmas) message.

America already had a film star as president when it elected Ronald Reagan. This time, they chose a reality TV star, the big-gun host of *The Apprentice*. As you know, the show, produced and hosted by Trump himself, features budding entrepreneurs who compete with each other on a series of tasks. One contestant is eliminated at the end of each show until just two are left. Trump then chooses the winner, who is offered a senior post in one of his companies. Aside from the fact that the contestants had to use every trick in the book to get the others eliminated and save their own skins, the most enjoyable moment in the show was when the lame duck was symbolically executed on live TV, as Trump barked "You're fired!" from his position of absolute authority ensconced in a large dark red office chair. Half avenging God, half absolute monarch.

"You're fired": in his first year in office, Trump became the biggest boss of them all, wielding his superiority and getting rid of anyone whose performance (or face) he didn't like. By April 2018, a little over a year since taking over the White House, Trump had seen off no fewer than 22 senior staff; five of them were "fired" and the others resigned of their own volition. The most notable was FBI director James Comey, fired by Trump while investigating possible links between

Trump's campaign team and Russia. Nothing seems to give him greater pleasure than being in a position to choose symbolic life or death for his entourage, or even the whole of the human race. Not even symbolic, now that I come to think of it: when he first took on the North Korean leader Kim Jong Un, before their hostility turned into "love," he openly boasted, "I too have a Nuclear Button, but it is a much bigger & more powerful one than his, and my Button works!"[45]

45. Whenever Trump boasts about the size of his ... power, it's tempting to see it as a slightly desperate display of virility. Like when he said he had "big, beautiful hands. Look at these hands!" Or at the September 26, 2018 press conference when he said: "China has total respect for Donald Trump and for Donald Trump's very, very large brain."

What He Doesn't Say

Trump doesn't talk all the time. Or rather he does, but there are things he doesn't say. And what Trump leaves unspoken is still Trump.

For instance, he doesn't use complicated words. He doesn't utter complex sentences. (That wasn't always the case. According to *The Atlantic*, his speech capacity has declined considerably. The magazine quotes Ben Michaelis, a psychologist specializing in language issues, who argues that Trump has exhibited "a clear reduction in linguistic sophistication over time," with "simpler word choices and sentence structure."[46] *The Atlantic* suggests these could be early symptoms of Alzheimer's disease, as was the case for former president Reagan.) He doesn't quote classic authors. He doesn't make ironic jokes.

Nor does he apologize. Not for making fun of war hero John McCain's time in captivity in Vietnam. Nor for calling Mexicans rapists. Nor for calling various African countries and Haiti shitholes. Nor for mocking a disabled reporter. Yet there can be no doubt he knows what apologies are: he's constantly demanding them from other people. "Fake News is at an all time high. Where is their apology to me for all of the incorrect stories ???" (June 13, 2017). To date he has apologized twice, and each time it was perfectly obvious he didn't mean a word of it: once because he had no choice, and the other because it was politically expedient. The first was late in his election campaign, after publication of the video where he can be heard talking about grabbing women by the pussy: "I said it, I was wrong, I apologize," he said in a video response. He went on to explain that he's still a pretty great guy compared to Bill Clinton, who "has actually abused women and

46. James Hamblin, "Is Something Neurologically Wrong With Donald Trump?" *The Atlantic* (January 3, 2018).

Hillary has bullied, attacked, shamed and intimidated his victims." His apology was enough to earn forgiveness from those of his future voters who might have been shocked by his words.

The second apology came in October 2018, after the Senate confirmed Brett Kavanaugh's Supreme Court membership following weeks of tension over the accusations of sexual assault leveled against him. Trump, who had already spoken of his confidence in Kavanaugh and other Republicans because he "never saw them do anything wrong,"[47] publicly apologized to Kavanaugh at his swearing-in ceremony: "You, sir, under historic scrutiny, were proven innocent" after "a campaign of political and personal destruction based on lies and deception."

The subtext is that all of the women who accused Kavanaugh were lying. Of course these apologies were not sincere — they were a way for Trump to gloat over some of the people he hates the most: women who speak out against abuse and the media that gives them airtime. Kavanaugh's innocence or otherwise was beside the point: Trump's ersatz apology, taking the Senate's ratification of his nominee to clear his name totally, was an opportunity to relish his triumph and deal a body-blow to anyone who disagreed with the truth spoken by Trump himself and his camp.

More deafening silence came in 2017 following the tragic events in Charlottesville. On August 12, white supremacists were demonstrating against the removal of a statue of General Robert E. Lee. One of them rammed his car into a crowd of anti-racism protestors, killing 32-year-old Heather Heyer and injuring seventeen others. In the wake of this tragedy, Trump held a press conference to condemn the "egregious display of hatred, bigotry and violence on many sides."

47. At the press conference on September 26, 2018, in response to a reporter who asked him if he had ever given the benefit of the doubt to a woman.

Many Americans were indignant at his failure to condemn the white supremacists who had organized the protest. When this silence prompted outrage, it took him two days to come out with a statement against racism, supremacists, and the KKK. "Racism is evil," he declared, really going out on a limb and breaking new ground.[48]

But nature will out: a few days later, meeting with reporters, he couldn't help but point out that the white supremacists had authorization for their protest, not the anti-racists, and there were "very fine people" on both sides.

Trump's silence, interpreted as a refusal to take a stand against neo-Nazis, was a perfectly clear message. Translated into the European context, his policies and positions are on the far right: xenophobia, isolationism, pro-death penalty, constant scapegoating of foreigners, rejection of supranational bodies, ostentatious displays of admiration for the firm hand of today's dictators — sounds like a regular chat round the Le Pen dinner table.[49] The American alt-right has come out for him and used his 2016 election as a springboard to a more central place in American political discourse. It's not a nice thing to say, but America is led by a man who, judged by European standards, is what someone less polite than me might call an outright fascist.

48. According to Bob Woodward (*Fear: Trump in the White House, op. cit.*), it was his staff secretary Rob Porter who convinced him to speak out against the racists. Trump let himself be persuaded but later thought this was a mistake: "That was the biggest fucking mistake I've made. You never make those concessions. You never apologize. I didn't do anything wrong in the first place. Why look weak?"

49. Translator's note: Jean-Marie Le Pen (b. 1928) was president of the far-right Front National party from 1972 to 2011, when his daughter Marine Le Pen (b. 1968) took over. She faced Emmanuel Macron in the run-off for the 2017 presidential election but lost by a wide margin. Various other members of the extended Le Pen family are also active in the party, now renamed the Rassemblement National.

End Game

Many of Trump's opponents dream fervently, but impotently, of ousting him. Many Democrats have fond hopes of impeachment.[50] At the time of writing, halfway through his mandate, nothing suggests that the procedure is justified. And in the end, I'm not sure it even matters.

Because in the end, the problem is not Donald Trump. His language, his manner of speaking or *not* speaking, the coarseness or otherwise of his words, are merely a tiny tree hiding a vast forest planted the day the pilgrims hopped off the *Mayflower* and set about destroying and rebuilding America with genocide and forced Christianization as their stock in trade.[51]

There is a collective responsibility. Trumpspeak perfectly reflects his thinking and his politics, imbued with vulgarity, misogyny, racism, financial greed, and a wholesale lack of empathy because it has grown out of his times and his society. When America looks at its president, it sees itself in what it thinks is a fun-house mirror. What it really sees, however, is a reality that it has long swept under the carpet. America is now paying the price.

The American dream was only ever that — a *dream*. Trump's slogan, "Make America Great Again," is rooted in a fantasy that was never destined to become reality, though other hopefuls running for office have used it before. America's most glittering promises have always been driven by aspirations that are far less

50. Translator's note: the French book dates from before the impeachment proceedings.

51. Yes, that is what America is symbolically built on. The first settlers were Puritans fleeing persecution in Europe & who found in the New World either a sudden, violent death, or the opportunity to become the persecutors in turn in the name of Christian morality, whose traces remain highly visible to this day.

glorious than the myths of American history suggest. Of course, America is not alone in this: here in France, we sing the praises of democracy and boast about the Revolution and Napoleon, while hastening to forget that the great historical advances we are so proud of were drenched in blood and, in most cases, driven by individuals who placed their own economic and political interests ahead of their fellow men — but who understood the importance of making it *look* good so that everyone believed it was for the best.[52]

In the United States, a country built on the blood of the indigenous peoples, imported African slaves, and pioneers promised the moon on a stick, the success of a minority filled the national imagination and crowded out the suffering of entire swathes of the population. It is true that America has afforded some the opportunity to make it big from humble beginnings: the Rockefellers, Carnegies, and the Bill Gates of this world. But America is also the land of immigrants who arrived with heads full of dreams and empty bellies, who never found their gold, oil, or genius start-up idea. It is the land of white trash, Native Americans dumped on reservations, slaves and their descendants, segregation for Blacks, lynching, and — still — racism that refuses to die.

The American dream was and is out of reach for many, many men & women, despite the national iconography full to bursting with misleading symbolism. Alongside the pilgrims coming to practice their religion in peace, the settlers merrily crossing the great plains in their covered wagons (hey there, Laura Ingalls Wilder), Western saloons full of good-time girls, GIs kissing French beauties after liberating Paris,

---

52. To take the examples that we Frenchies are proudest of: the French Revolution was a dirty business that took many innocent lives, even before you get to the Terror. And Napoleon was a nutcase driven mad by ambition who dreamed of conquering all of Europe.

the reality is that the pilgrims died of hunger and disease or slaughtered the native Americans (who, to be fair, did what they could to slaughter the settlers, but we all know who won). The settlers, promised untold riches by the government for driving the natives from their lands to help the train companies expand from coast to coast, died in their thousands of starvation and exhaustion as they pushed the frontier westwards. Many were scalped. The bloody civil war freed the slaves but also led to the KKK and segregationist laws. Those brave GIs were soon to die in their thousands in Vietnam, and to this day nobody quite knows what the point was.

Now, you might say this is an overly simplistic, black-and-white version of American history and that it was much more complicated than that. Well, that may be true, but that is the vision of America that voters are being sold today.

"Make America Great Again" is an invitation to return to a past that never existed, a simple, right-vs.-wrong world invoked by the either/or vision of American history not only in Trumpspeak, but also across the nation. On both sides of the debate.

Faced with this portrait of Dorian Gray, America is clinging to its blinkers with all its might. As long as the United States refuses to name the root cause of their malaise and draw a line under a past they cherish to the point it cannot be called into question, they will not be able to drag themselves out of the swamp they have been mired in since Trump took office. Trump's presidency is merely symbolic of the quagmire.

Because someone else could be next. The malaise is not caused by just one man. The harm has been done, and now the floodgates stand wide open. Trump is not an accident of American history. We can't just turn the page once he leaves office: he will have made his mark not just in his policy decisions and his Supreme Court appointments, but across the whole of American society, which bears a collective responsibility for voting him into power — his direct voters for the main part, obviously, but also the political structure dating back generations that laid the groundwork for his victory. Just as dictatorships are built on a system, the United States crowned their forty-fifth president on a mountain of denial, rooted in communication, discourse — in *language*.

Trump is not the worst problem facing America. The president is the guarantor of America's moral order, the nation's symbolic superego. He is supposed to be a model and a yardstick for the nation's morality. When the president speaks out against an act of hatred, America stands behind him. But when he chooses to remain silent, or worse, to implicitly encourage violence, institutional or individual, he gives *carte blanche* to the disturbed, the hate-filled, who hold their lowest instincts in check as long as they know their acts of aggression will be censured by the highest office in the land, representing society as a whole. As Jacques Généreux writes in *L'Autre société*:

> In humans, aggressive instincts are regulated not genetically, but socially, by rituals & habits transmitted in our upbringing. Violent and anti-social behavior thus reflect a failure to learn the limits & the laws, and can arise from, or be aggravated by, a failure of the culture, conventions, and institutions that stipulate and legitimize taboo behaviors.[53]

The violence inherent in Trumpspeak and those who use it can be seen as legitimizing the use of violence and anti-social behavior by those who, prior to his election, might have stayed on the right side of the line. These people and their behavior will still be there after Trump's period in office, whether or not he serves a second mandate, and will leave a lasting trace across the strata of American society, for years to come.

---

53. *L'Autre société. À la recherche du progrès humain* (Paris: Le Seuil, 2011).

The founding act of semantic fraud is in fact the Declaration of Independence: "We hold these truths to be self-evident, that all men are created equal, that they are endowed by their Creator with certain un-alienable Rights, that among these are Life, Liberty and the pursuit of Happiness." Of course it's a noble aim couched in fine words, but you need to remember it was written by a slave owner whose new nation was squatting on land stolen from its former occupants. In writing the introduction to the Declaration of Independence, Jefferson was penning the opening lines of the American myth, the great dishonest dream that millions of people were to chase, in words that in no way reflected the reality that he and his contemporaries were living in. The Declaration of Independence was the first official statement of alt-reality. The first fake news in American history.

The First Amendment protects a whole host of freedoms, particularly freedom of worship and expression. In America, you're allowed to say and think whatever you want. You can walk around draped in swastikas and wish people dead in public or even in print. All within the constitution. Inciting racial hatred is not a crime. Holocaust denial is not a major taboo the way it is in France, where it is against the law to challenge the historical truth. In America, no one owns the truth. As a result, everyone has their own version of it and everyone can say whatever they like about where their own world came from and what it is like. Just like every other American, the president of the United States can say whatever he likes and tell people that it's the truth. Nothing in the language of the constitution is there as a crash barrier. So why *not* say that climate change doesn't exist, that coal is clean energy, or that your inauguration drew unprecedented crowds? It's not that much more out there than claiming Adam and Eve waded around in the primeval mud with the dinosaurs as the absolute literal truth, as many schools teach.[54] If you go back to the founding act of American politics, it is clear that the much venerated Founding Fathers gave *carte blanche* to the practice.

There is one sort of linguistic censorship widely applied in America, just one extraordinarily powerful interdiction shared widely across all social strata. It might even be the most widely held attitude in American society. In America you are free to say or write that Jews don't deserve to live, that Blacks are an inferior race, or that Mexicans are rapists, but there remains one semantic field that lies outside the national discourse. What you are *not* allowed to mention in America is a hangover from the nation's Puritan roots, Evil with a capital E, the scourge of society: sex.

America has such a problem with sex (just ask Woody Allen) that it would take a whole book to talk about it, which I won't, because it's time I wrapped this one up. But in just a few words, America's founding era — when sex had to be absolutely policed first by the religious authorities, and later by the state, when for women, sex was boiled right down to procreation, and for men, it was allowed as long as it remained a discreet, sin-tainted pleasure — gave rise to a society in which the sexual revolution and the progressive but as yet incomplete process of women claiming ownership of their bodies failed to blot out the stamp of evil still branded on sex outside the holy bonds of matrimony with a view to procreation.[55]

54. A 2014 Gallup poll found that 42% of Americans believed God created humans ten thousand years ago. Many American schools teach creationism in philosophy, religious studies, and civics classes, and some states such as Texas allow teachers to teach "alternatives" to evolution in biology classes.

55. I highly recommend you read, or re-read, Nathaniel Hawthorne's *Scarlet Letter*, about a young Puritan woman in 1640s America, condemned for adultery and branded with the letter A on her chest. Then read Margaret Atwood's *The Handmaid's Tale*, a dystopian novel describing a society in which women are reduced to a role as incubators. Then compare the two and see that some things have barely advanced in the past four centuries.

BÉRENGÈRE VIENNOT

But what's that got to do with anything? I hear you ask. Hang on, I'll get there in a moment. In America, in 2019, you can watch any kind of violence and warfare on any media you choose — cinema, television, or online. Almost anyone can buy a gun with a minimum of effort. But what you can't do is say anything sex-related, like "fuck" or "vagina," on television. To protect people's feelings. A bit like the Bible, which makes a virtue of violence and an anathema of sex.

In the course of writing this book, I watched hours and hours of videos of Trump, of course, and of American television in general — documentaries, TV news. When I was looking into Trump's reaction to the Charlottesville protests, I came across a CNN report. And I was shocked to see the car that drove into the crowd and killed Heather Heyer. I saw bodies thrown into the air and the car drive off, leaving behind a blood-soaked, screaming crowd.[56]

Whether this demonstration of violence was artistic, informative, purposeful, whatever, it was just one of millions of similar images shown daily on American media, no punches pulled. But none of them will let any sexual swear words sully their airwaves. *Those* words are replaced by a modest "beep" to protect delicate ears. OK, so it's a bit of a cliché to draw a parallel between the overt foregrounding of violence and the negation of sexuality. But the truth is sometimes obvious. What kind of behavior can we expect to see in a society that is constantly repressing sexual urges while giving free rein to aggressive impulses?

Without paging Dr. Freud, I think it's safe to say that a society that totally denies the importance, and

56. Spike Lee chose the scene to end his film *BlacKkKlansman*, splicing it with declarations by Trump that both sides had done wrong. This was the first film to show the extent to which the Trump era embodied an institutional regression in terms of race and social relations across America.

the omnipresence, of sexuality in healthy human behavior is doomed to trip up one way or another. Either
it is "puritanized" and considered solely as a moral
straitjacket (at least in public) by conservatives who
are usually against abortion, or it is excessively sexual-
ized (such as by artists and their super-sexualized cre-
ations) in a transgressive act of rebellion, like a teen-
ager acting out against being grounded.

*

America's new language, Trumpspeak, did not spring
wholly formed from the mouth of a billionaire with
no political background. It cannot be reduced to the
wild frothing of a man who we like to think of as completely insane, so that we can be excused from listening to what he has to say. No. We *must* listen to Donald
Trump, because he is not a stupid man: despite his
crushing lack of culture, by the sheer force of his ego
he has managed to conquer the highest office in modern human history.

We must listen to Donald Trump because he is
the voice of the most violent, most despicable, and
now the most powerful fringe of American society.
We must listen because the reign of Reason is over in
the West. The great gestures of international goodwill
that arose from the disaster of the First World War,
which shaped the entire twentieth century, the alliances
between great nations to ensure that the worst of humanity would never again gain the upper hand, the
collaborations between well-intentioned intellectuals
seeking to bring happiness to the greatest number and
advance the cause of humanity as best they could —
all on the scrap heap. And all because one country led
by a man whose superego seems to be permanently
out to lunch, as proven every time he opens his mouth,
lets its most violent fringes give free rein to their bas-
est instincts.

We must listen to Donald Trump, despite the powerful temptation to bask in the moral and intellectual superiority (real or imagined) that urges us to refuse to play his game and take him seriously. The Democratic intelligentsia paid a heavy price on November 8, 2016, for pointing & laughing when the reality TV star threw his hat in the ring to become a Washington heavyweight.

And we must listen to Donald Trump, because he is *contagious*. Violence is seeping into words and deeds in Brazil, Hungary, Turkey, Italy, Austria, and elsewhere. In these countries, which thought the lessons of history would keep them safe, more and more citizens are tuning into America and listening to Trumpspeak.

Acknowledgments

First and foremost, thanks to Clotilde Meyer, who sparked this book and guided me through it with considerable enthusiasm, efficiency, and kindness.

Thanks to you for reading these acknowledgments, though you're probably not in them.

Thanks to Bonnie and Josh, my greatest — and most objective — fans.

Thanks to everyone who became a psychological crutch for the months it took me to write this book: Inga Nop, my soul sister for a quarter of a century for her steadfast belief in me, Peggy Sastre for her biased yet active read-through of the manuscript, Anne-Laure Bell, Marie Aarnink, and Solène Sellier for musical & moral support, Chloé Leleu, my fellow slave to semantics, Alexandra Louis and Céline Griffon, the first to make me want to write during those endless hours of boredom at high school.

Last but not least, thanks to Romuald Serive, the unwitting trigger to my life as a writer.

Thanks to Susan Pickford, whose efforts & talent have allowed the book to exist in English.

*

The translator wishes to thank Ann Kaiser for helping bring the project to fruition.

COLOPHON

TRUMPSPEAK

was handset in InDesign CC in 2020

The text font is MT *Dante*
The display font is *Fakir Black*

Book design *&* typesetting: Emiliano Sangrado
Cover design: CMP
Cover illustration: Gerardo Paoletti
Opening spread drawing: Jason Alexander Byers

TRUMPSPEAK

is published by Contra Mundum Press.

Contra Mundum Press   New York · London · Melbourne

CONTRA MUNDUM PRESS

Dedicated to the value & the indispensable importance of the individual voice, to works that test the boundaries of thought & experience.

The primary aim of Contra Mundum is to publish translations of writers who in their use of form and style are *à rebours*, or who deviate significantly from more programmatic & spurious forms of experimentation. Such writing attests to the volatile nature of modernism. Our preference is for works that have not yet been translated into English, are out of print, or are poorly translated, for writers whose thinking & æsthetics are in opposition to timely or mainstream currents of thought, value systems, or moralities. We also reprint obscure and out-of-print works we consider significant but which have been forgotten, neglected, or overshadowed.

There are many works of fundamental significance to *Weltliteratur* (& *Weltkultur*) that still remain in relative oblivion, works that alter and disrupt standard circuits of thought — these warrant being encountered by the world at large. It is our aim to render them more visible.

For the complete list of forthcoming publications, please visit our website. To be added to our mailing list, send your name & email address to: info@contramundum.net

Contra Mundum Press
P.O. Box 1326
New York, NY 10276
USA

OTHER CONTRA MUNDUM PRESS TITLES

THE FUTURE OF KULCHUR
A PATRONAGE PROJECT

LEND CONTRA MUNDUM PRESS (CMP) YOUR SUPPORT

With bookstores and presses around the world struggling to survive, and many actually closing, we are forming this patronage project as a means for establishing a continuous & stable foundation to safeguard our longevity. Through this patronage project we would be able to remain free of having to rely upon government support &/or other official funding bodies, not to speak of their timelines & impositions. It would also free CMP from suffering the vagaries of the publishing industry, as well as the risk of submitting to commercial pressures in order to persist, thereby potentially compromising the integrity of our catalog.

CAN YOU SACRIFICE $10 A WEEK FOR KULCHUR?

For the equivalent of merely 2–3 coffees a week, you can help sustain CMP and contribute to the future of kulchur. To participate in our patronage program we are asking individuals to donate $500 per year, which amounts to $42/month, or $10/week. Larger donations are of course welcome and beneficial. All donations are tax-deductible through our fiscal sponsor Fractured Atlas. If preferred, donations can be made in two installments. We are seeking a minimum of 300 patrons per year and would like for them to commit to giving the above amount for a period of three years.

Part tax-deductible donation, part exchange, for your contribution you will receive every CMP book published during the patronage period as well as 20 books from our back catalog. When possible, signed or limited editions of books will be offered as well.

WHAT WILL CMP DO WITH YOUR CONTRIBUTIONS?

Your contribution will help with basic general operating expenses, yearly production expenses (book printing, warehouse & catalog fees, etc.), advertising & outreach, and editorial, proofreading, translation, typography, design and copyright fees. Funds may also be used for participating in book fairs and staging events. Additionally, we hope to rebuild the *Hyperion* section of the website in order to modernize it.

From Pericles to Mæcenas & the Renaissance patrons, it is the magnanimity of such individuals that have helped the arts to flourish. Be a part of helping your kulchur flourish; be a part of history.

HOW

To lend your support & become a patron, please visit the subscription page of our website: contramundum.net/subscription

For any questions, write us at: info@contramundum.net